Refinishing & Finishing Wood

Cy DeCosse Incorporated
Minnetonka, Minnesota

Contents

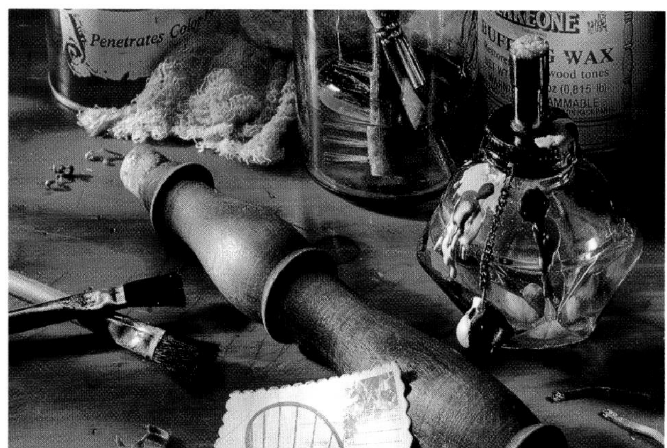

Introduction **5**

Why Refinish? 6
Refinishing Wood:
A Step-by-step Overview 12

Evaluating & Planning **15**

Evaluating Furniture 17
Evaluating Wood Floors 20
Evaluating Woodwork 21
Identifying Old Finishes 22
Selecting a New Finish 24
Tools for Refinishing 28
Safety, Cleanup & Disposal 30

Copyright © 1994
Cy DeCosse Incorporated
5900 Green Oak Drive
Minnetonka, Minnesota 55343
1-800-328-3895
All rights reserved
Printed in U.S.A.

Also available from the publisher:
Everyday Home Repairs, Decorating With Paint & Wallcovering, Carpentry: Tools • Shelves • Walls • Doors, Building Decks, Kitchen Remodeling, Home Plumbing Projects & Repairs, Basic Wiring & Electrical Repairs, Workshop Tips & Techniques, Advanced Home Wiring, Carpentry: Remodeling, Landscape Design & Construction, Bathroom Remodeling, Built-In Projects for the Home, Exterior Home Repairs & Improvements, Home Masonry Repairs & Projects

Library of Congress
Cataloging-in-Publication Data

Refinishing & finishing wood

p. cm.—(Black & Decker home improvement library)
Includes index.
ISBN 0-86573-739-8 (hardcover).
ISBN 0-86573-740-1 (softcover).
1. Wood refinishing. 2. Furniture refinishing.
3. Floors, Wooden.
I. Cy DeCosse Incorporated.
II. Title: Refinishing and finishing wood.
III. Series.
TT325.R38 1994
698'.3—dc20 94-30079

CY DeCOSSE INCORPORATED

A COWLES MAGAZINES COMPANY

Chairman/CEO: Bruce Barnet
Chairman Emeritus: Cy DeCosse
President/COO: Nino Tarantino
Executive V.P./Editor-in-Chief: William B. Jones

Created by: The editors of Cy DeCosse Incorporated, in cooperation with Black & Decker. BLACK&DECKER is a trademark of the Black & Decker Corporation and is used under license.

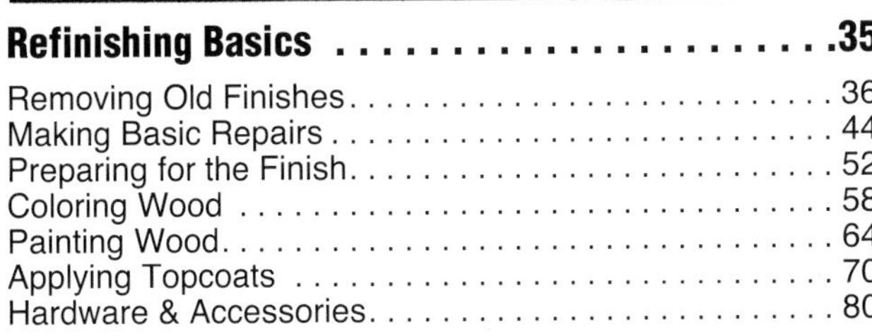

Refinishing Basics .35

Removing Old Finishes . . . 36
Making Basic Repairs . . . 44
Preparing for the Finish . . . 52
Coloring Wood . . . 58
Painting Wood . . . 64
Applying Topcoats . . . 70
Hardware & Accessories . . . 80

Case Studies . . . 84

Rocking Chair . . . 88
Sewing Machine Cabinet . . . 90
Kitchen Cabinets . . . 92
Dining Chair . . . 94
Chest of Drawers . . . 96
School Desks . . . 98
Frame-and-panel Cabinet . . . 100
Cedar Chest . . . 102
Antique Mantel Clock . . . 104
Tip-Top Table . . . 106
Music Cabinet . . . 108
Antique Radio Console . . . 110
Double-hung Window . . . 112
Woodwork & Door . . . 114
Wood Floor . . . 118

Maintenance & Quick Fixes . . . 122

Index . . . 126

Project Director: Paul Currie
Project Manager: Diane Dreon
Senior Editor: Mark Johanson
Editors: Carol Harvatin, Jim Huntley, Jon Simpson
Senior Art Director: Tim Himsel
Art Directors: John Hermansen, Dave Schelitzche, Gina Seeling
Technical Production Editor: Gary Sandin
Assistant Technical Production Editor: Greg Pluth
Vice President of Development Planning & Production: Jim Bindas
Copy Editor: Janice Cauley
Contributing Editors: Anne Price, Bryan Trandem

Shop Supervisor: Phil Juntti
Set Builders: Rob Johnstone, John Nadeau, Mike Peterson, Greg Wallace
Print Production Manager: Laurie Gilbert
Production Staff: Kevin Hedden, Mike Hehner, Jeanette Moss, Robert Powers, Mike Schauer, Kay Wethern, Nik Wogstad
Director of Photography: Mike Parker
Creative Photo Coordinator: Cathleen Shannon
Studio Manager: Marcia Chambers
Lead Photographer: Mark Macemon
Photographers: Stewart Block, Rebecca Hawthorne, Mike Hehner, Rex Irmen, William Lindner, Paul Najlis, Chuck Nields, Mike Parker

Contributing Photographers: Kim Bailey, Doug Deutscher, Paul Markert, Mette Nielsen, Brad Parker

Contributing Manufacturers: The Bartley Collection, Ltd.; Klean-Strip, a division of WM Barr

Printed on American paper by: Quebecor Graphics
99 98 97 96 / 5 4 3 2 1

Made from natural wood
6 MAHOG
Penetrates Color
LES PRODUITS DES ANCIENS EBENISTES
LAKEONE
PARIS 1902
WAX
wood tones
oz (0,815 lb)

Introduction

An old rocking chair, a well-used cedar chest, a hardwood floor that has lost its luster—anywhere you look around your home, you are likely to find a potential refinishing project. But even the most ardent do-it-yourselfers often draw the line at refinishing. They have a vision of refinishing that is filled with messy, harsh chemicals and endless sanding and scraping. In reality, refinishing and finishing wood is a manageable process that can yield professional-quality results with surprisingly little mess and fuss if you use the right tools and techniques.

Refinishing furniture is an adventure. It begins in attics, antique stores, or at garage sales; usually with the question, "Wouldn't that look nice if...?" And the more involved you become in a project, the more questions you encounter: How can I unlock the potential of that old sewing cabinet? What is the best way to sand the grooves on a rocking chair spindle? Should I use chemicals or a heat gun to remove the old finish on my antique clock?

Refinishing & Finishing Wood gives you all the information you need to bring new life and a lasting finish to furniture, floors, and woodwork. It takes you through every phase of the refinishing and finishing process: evaluating old furniture and finishes to develop a refinishing strategy; making minor repairs like filling gouges and regluing joints; removing an old finish with a heat gun or chemical stripper; finish sanding and filling wood grain; coloring and topcoating new and stripped wood; revamping hardware and other accessories; and more.

We also give you the most up-to-date information on new refinishing and finishing products that are safer to use and safer for the environment. Disposal, safety, and cleanup issues are examined in detail.

As a special bonus, *Refinishing & Finishing Wood* contains a section featuring 15 separate case studies that take the mystery out of refinishing. The section leads you step-by-step through the refinishing process, providing insight into the decisions that make any project a success. You will find clear examples addressing the same challenges you are facing—and offering solutions for meeting those challenges.

From cleaning a dirty wax finish, to repairing, stripping, sanding, and refinishing an old piece of furniture, the skills you learn in *Refinishing & Finishing Wood* are do-it-yourself abilities that you will use again and again to add value and restore beauty to your worn-but-sturdy woodwork and furniture.

NOTICE TO READERS

This book provides useful instructions, but we cannot anticipate all of your working conditions or the characteristics of your materials and tools. For safety, you should use caution, care, and good judgment when following the procedures described in this book. Consider your own skill level and the instructions and safety precautions associated with the various tools and materials shown. Neither the publisher nor Black & Decker® can assume responsibility for any damage to property or injury to persons as a result of misuse of the information provided.

The instructions in this book conform to "The Uniform Plumbing Code," "The National Electrical Code Reference Book," and "The Uniform Building Code" current at the time of its original publication. Consult your local Building Department for information on building permits, codes, and other laws as they apply to your project.

Why Refinish?

Refinishing wood is more than just another do-it-yourself skill. Practical skills like carpentry, plumbing, or wiring help you save money and make sure your home improvements are done the right way. But giving new life to an old rocking chair by transforming it from an eyesore to a centerpiece gives you a special sense of satisfaction.

Studies have shown that most people who have made a hobby of refinishing are not in it for any kind of financial advantage. They do it because it is fun. A successful refinishing project brings out the artist, historian, and the creative caretaker in even the most practical-minded do-it-yourselfer. Most people who successfully complete one refinishing project become hooked—they enjoy it enough to take on additional projects.

Beyond the feelings of fun and pride inspired by the process, there are many practical benefits to refinishing and finishing wood. A well-executed refinishing job can increase the value of a worn-out article. Buying fine furniture in the rough and refinishing it is an inexpensive way to decorate your home. And refinishing old furniture is an excellent form of recycling—not only does it eliminate the disposal problem, it also preserves resources that would be used to create a replacement.

A new finish makes your favorite old furniture last longer by protecting it from moisture, heat, and spills. Increasing your understanding of wood finishes gives you all the background you need to properly maintain and care for wood.

Restore lost beauty. A new finish and a few new accessories give fresh life to a forgotten piece of furniture. Pages 110 to 111.

Uncover buried treasure. A plain painted cabinet is unmasked to reveal fine furniture. Pages 90 to 91.

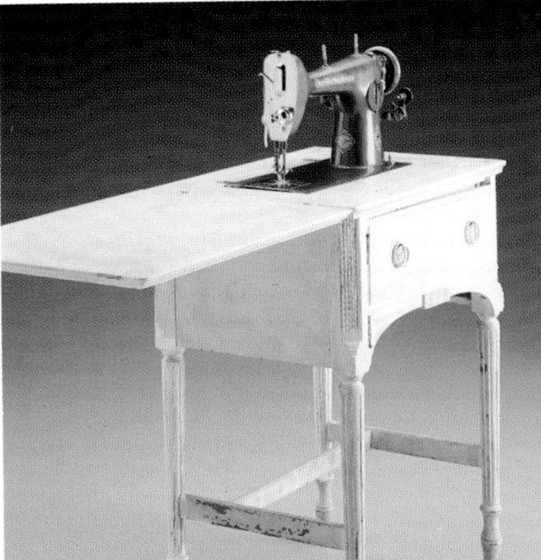

Unleash potential. A chair plagued by loose joints and layers of old paint is transformed into a classic American antique. Pages 88 to 89.

Why Refinish?

Put a fine finish on new wood. An unfinished, kit-built table gets a first-class finish treatment. Pages 106 to 107.

Make the ordinary extraordinary. A plain pine dresser gets a serious sprucing up. Pages 96 to 97.

Extend a life.
A cedar chest confined to basement storage duty becomes a showpiece.
Pages 102 to 103.

Turn darkness into light.
An old, dirty finish is eliminated, and bright wood tones come shining through.
Pages 108 to 109.

Why Refinish?

Make time for fun.
A quick cleanup and some creativity excite the imagination and save a valuable antique.
Pages 104 to 105.

Step out in style.
A frame-and-panel cabinet is dressed up to showcase its distinctive styling.
Pages 100 to 101.

Make a house a home. Refinished floors, woodwork, and doors brighten a dreary room. Pages 114 to 121.

Refinishing Wood: A Step-by-step Overview

This overview sequence shows the basic how-to steps in a major refinishing project—from evaluating potential projects to attaching the last piece of hardware. Your own refinishing or finishing project may require all these steps, or perhaps only a few. To help determine which steps your planned project requires—and how to accomplish them—browse through the *Case Studies* section at the end of this book (pages 84 to 123).

Evaluate the potential project before you start (pages 16 to 23). Look for good wood, solid construction and other signs that indicate a strong likelihood of success.

How to Refinish Wood: a Step-by-step Overview

1 Remove the old finish (pages 36 to 43). Heat stripping, chemical stripping, and sanding are the primary methods for removing an old finish. Most projects require more than one removal method.

2 Make basic repairs (pages 44 to 51). Fixing problems, like the loose stretchers we reglued here, ensures that your completed project will be sturdy as well as beautiful.

3 Prepare for the finish (pages 52 to 57). Fixing flaws like dents and gouges then thoroughly finish sanding are essential steps in creating a smooth surface suitable for staining and topcoating.

4 Color the wood (pages 58 to 63). Use penetrating oil or stain to enrich a grain pattern, create a pleasing color, or even to hide flaws in the wood. In some cases, paint is used instead of stain for a more decorative appearance (pages 64 to 69). Or, you may prefer to skip the wood-coloring step altogether and let the natural color and beauty of the wood speak for itself.

5 Apply a topcoat (pages 70 to 79). A hard, clear finish layer applied over the wood protects it from moisture and scratches, seals in the color, and adds depth to the finish.

6 Complete the project (pages 80 to 83). Refurbish or replace hardware and other accessories to provide the final touch to a refinishing project.

Evaluating & Planning

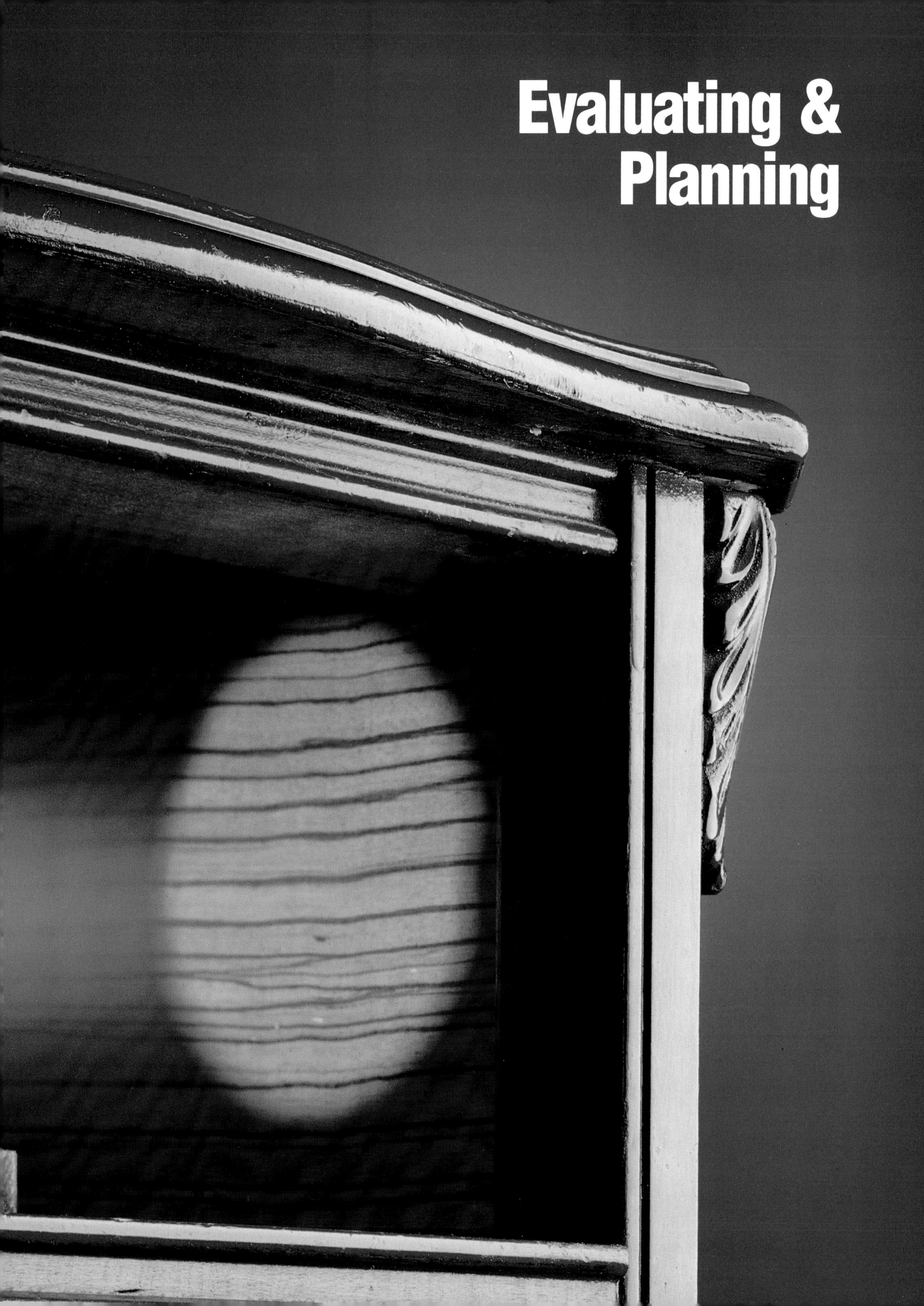

Removing hardware and other accessories from painted furniture and woodwork can provide useful information about the old finish and the type and condition of the wood.

Evaluating & Planning

Potential refinishing projects can be found in virtually every home, garage, and antique store. But the fact that a piece of furniture or a floor is old or worn out does not necessarily make it a good candidate for refinishing. The wood could be damaged beyond repair, or the finish may be too stubborn to be removed completely. Many times, stripping a piece of furniture only reveals that the paint was there for a reason—to cover damaged or unattractive wood. But for every project that is a risky refinishing choice, there is another that has the possibility of great success. Learning to distinguish between a wise choice and a waste of time is simply a matter of knowing what to look for.

This section shows you some warning signs and some indicators of good potential. We tell you how to estimate what certain problems mean in terms of time, expense, and likelihood of success. But the ultimate decision on whether or not to proceed with a project is up to you: keep in mind that sometimes the most ill-advised project turns out wonderfully—especially if it has sentimental value to the refinisher.

Once you have chosen a refinishing or finishing project, make a plan. Having a new finish in mind helps you make decisions, like choosing a finish-removal method, or determining how thoroughly to sand the wood. Once you decide what repairs need to be made, for example, you can more accurately estimate the time commitment and cost of the project. But stay flexible when planning. Refinishing is full of surprises, and plans inevitably require modification as you learn more about your project.

This section shows:

- Evaluating Furniture (pages17 to 19)
- Evaluating Wood Floors (page 20)
- Evaluating Woodwork (page 21)
- Identifying Old Finishes (pages 22 to 23)
- Selecting a New Finish (pages 24 to 27)
- Tools for Refinishing (pages 28 to 29)
- Safety, Cleanup & Disposal (pages 30 to 33)

Evaluating Furniture

Evaluating potential furniture refinishing projects is basically a four-step process: 1) study the wood to identify the type and assess its general condition; 2) evaluate structural soundness and identify needed repairs; 3) evaluate the condition of the wood surfaces to determine if an attractive finish is possible; 4) evaluate the condition of the finish to decide if it needs to be stripped off, or if cleaning and a few quick fixes will bring it back to life.

Also consider the age and value of the potential project. If it is a valuable antique, you probably should not choose it as your first refinishing experiment.

Based on your evaluation, make a decision about the project: is the final result likely to be worth the effort?

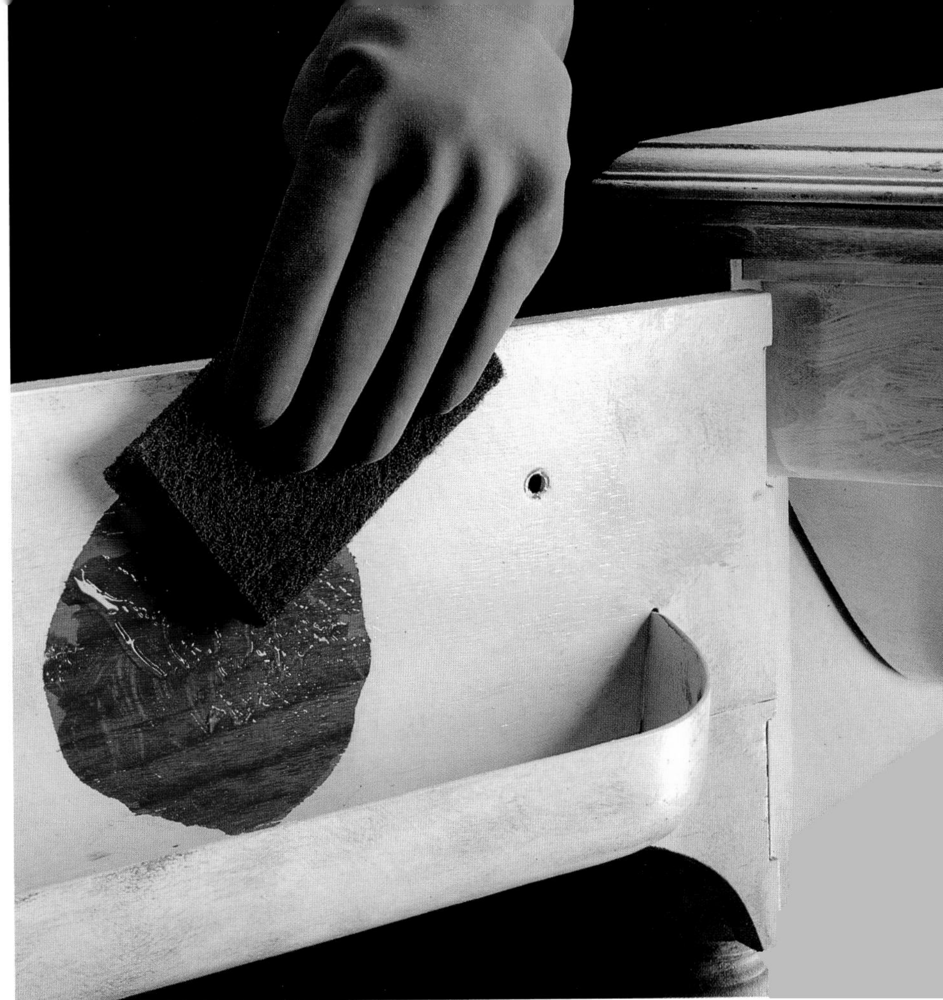

Remove a spot of finish in an inconspicuous area to examine the wood more closely.

Tips for Evaluating Furniture

Look for written clues like a manufacturer's name, a date, or a place of origin, to help you establish the age, value, and finish type. In some cases, a previous owner may have left a clue behind, like a receipt, an old piece of newspaper lining a drawer, or a note detailing the history of the piece. If you suspect the potential project is an antique, have it appraised by a professional before you do anything with it.

Examine hidden areas for information about the wood and the quality of the workmanship. Examining this dresser drawer, for example, revealed hand-cut dovetail joints that were still sturdy after more than 100 years of wear—sure signs the dresser was built with care. NOTE: There may be several types of wood in a single piece of furniture, so do not base all your conclusions on just one area.

How to Evaluate Potential Refinishing Projects

1 Evaluate the wood. The type of wood used in a piece of furniture has a great effect on its value and its suitability as a refinishing project. The two cabinets shown above are about the same size and they use the same type of joinery, but the similarities end there. One cabinet (left) looks old and battered, but it is made of sturdy hardwood, so the chances of reviving it are good. The other (right) is built from particleboard so, despite the presence of hardwood veneer, its prospects of withstanding a refinishing job are not good. Because the joints are sturdy, however, it is a good candidate for painting.

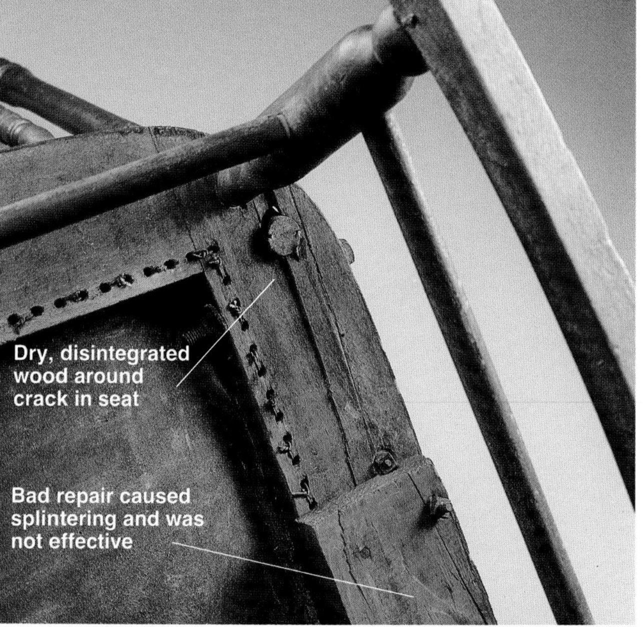

2 Evaluate the structural soundness. If a potential project is plagued with many loose joints and has obviously been repaired in the past, then there is a basic structural problem with the piece. The two pressback rocking chairs above each show signs of wear. One chair (left) has a crack in the seat that will require some repair, but the wood around the crack and at the joints is solid. A few repairs have been attempted already, but they have not caused any major problems, so the chair likely can be reclaimed. The other rocker (right) also has a cracked seat, but the wood has degenerated around the damaged area, and ineffective repair efforts caused further splintering and damage to the wood. Because the seat would have to be replaced, refinishing the rocker is probably not worth the effort.

3 Evaluate the condition of the wood surfaces. A few surface problems, including small dents and cracks (left), loose veneer (center), or small burns (right), all can be remedied easily. A few such problems should not disqualify a project from consideration. But making too many surface repairs will add considerably to the time the project requires, and you may well be disappointed with the result—disguising surface repairs, especially those requiring wood putty, is a very tricky job. With newer, solid wood furniture, however, you may be able to resurface flat surfaces that are in poor condition using a belt sander (pages 102 to 103).

4 Evaluate the condition of the finish. It is a mistake to assume that just because the finish looks worn it needs to be replaced. Especially on antique furniture, removing the old finish can cause significant devaluation. A few finish blemishes, like water stains (left), can be treated easily with the right techniques (pages 124 to 125), preserving the old finish. More severe finish problems, like alligatored shellac (center) usually require full finish removal. The original finish color also should be considered. Dark finishes (right) are normally absorbed deep into the wood, so if your goal is to create a very light finish, plan on plenty of sanding.

Remove layers of wax and grime so you can see the true condition of floor. Often, a simple cleaning with mineral spirits is all the "refinishing" a floor needs.

Evaluating Wood Floors

The condition of your floorboards is the primary factor in deciding if refinishing will be successful. Look for signs of rot, especially around pipes, radiators, and windows. Replacing floorboards is hard work, and getting a good match is difficult. Also check for dips or valleys, especially in high-traffic areas. Evaluate the overall evenness of the floors—roll a golf ball or marble across the floor in several spots and see how it behaves. Visually, uneven floors may not seem like a big problem, but they are next-to-impossible to sand because floor sanders do not follow dips and valleys.

If your floor is fairly even and fundamentally sound, your next step is to decide whether to resurface or chemically strip the old finish. Many homeowners have come to equate "doing your floors" with sanding the surface down to bare wood, but often chemical stripping is a more efficient method that yields better results. With uneven floors, parquet floors, veneered flooring products, and floors that have already been resurfaced, your only do-it-yourself refinishing option is to chemically strip the finish. Resurface floors only if many scratches, gouges, and stains have affected the floorboards.

Tips for Evaluating Wood Floors

Identify the type of flooring product. Standard 1"-thick hardwood floorboards can withstand one or two resurfacing projects with a drum sander, but some newer flooring products can only be chemically stripped—they simply do not have enough wood to withstand resurfacing. Sanding parquet flooring requires special sanders and is a job for professionals. Otherwise, it should be chemically stripped.

Look for signs of past resurfacing. Inexperienced floor refinishers often remove much more wood than is necessary when they power-sand a floor. Look near baseboards and radiators for sanding ridges where the power sander could not reach. If sanding ridges are visible, you probably do not have enough wood remaining above the tongues in tongue-and-groove floorboards to allow you to sand the floors again.

Evaluating Woodwork

Evaluating woodwork to determine its suitability for refinishing is a more complicated issue than evaluating floors. Condition of the wood certainly is important—you should examine it closely for signs of deterioration or extensive damage. Woodwork is often milled from softer wood types than floors, making it more susceptible to gouging, splintering, and decay. The fact that woodwork was painted often indicates that it has undergone repairs, or that some of the woodwork is not original and will be difficult to blend in.

When evaluating woodwork, note the intricateness of the trim pieces, particularly above doors, and check for detailed architectural millwork. Stripping an old finish from detailed woodwork can be a very time-consuming process. Test the woodwork in a few spots to find out if it can be removed easily for refinishing. For many people this is the most workable option—sending woodwork out for commercial stripping is a common practice. Refinishing woodwork in place is perhaps the easier option, but it can create quite a mess, and is physically demanding. Ask yourself if you are up to the task physically before you commit to refinishing woodwork in place.

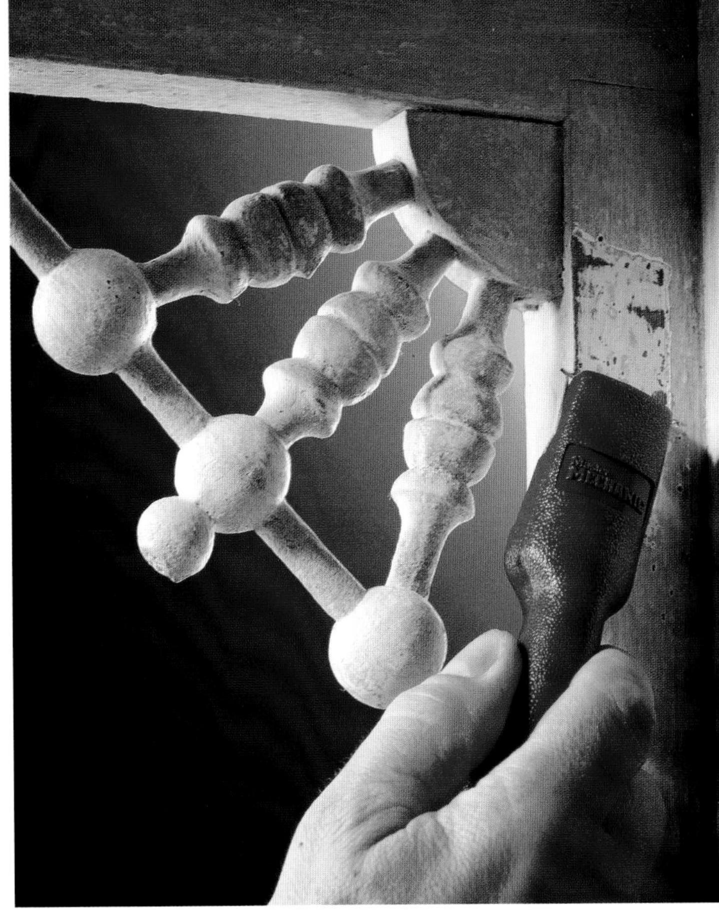

Check for paint in the first finish layer. If the first layer is paint, stripping the wood down to the natural wood color is very difficult. Painting is your best option.

Tips for Evaluating Woodwork

Carefully remove one piece of woodwork and check the back side to identify the wood type. Also examine the ends of the piece to see how thick the finish is and how deeply it has penetrated into the wood. You may even want to try stripping the piece to assess how easily the finish comes off. Also, if the piece was easy to remove, consider the option of removing all the woodwork for refinishing.

Test the condition of the wood. Probe the woodwork with a sharp instrument, especially around windows and other areas where moisture is present. Badly rotted woodwork should be replaced. Minor damage can be treated with wood-hardening products, but this option generally forces you to paint the woodwork. Some manufacturers, however, have introduced stainable wood hardener—ask at your local building center.

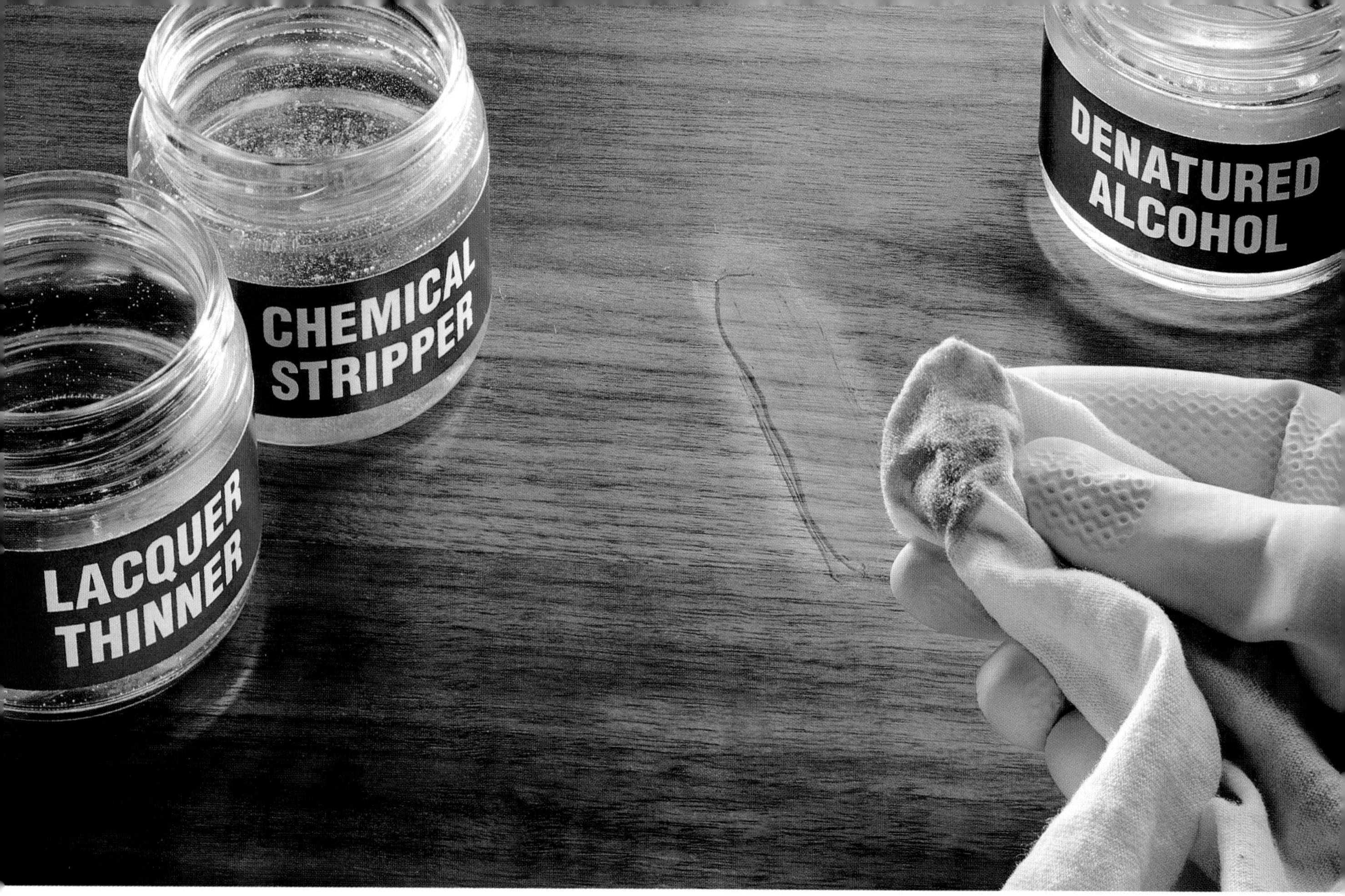

Test the old finish with solvents to identify the topcoat material. Dip a clean rag in the solvent you are testing, dab it onto the finish, then look for finish residue on the rag (make sure to give the chemical enough time to work). Always wipe the surface lightly with mineral spirits first to remove any wax buildup.

Identifying Old Finishes

Identifying the original topcoat material is an important stage in both the evaluation and the planning processes. It helps you estimate how much work is involved in removing the topcoat. Knowing the type of topcoat also helps determine your options for restoring the workpiece—some finishes are easier to repair than others, and depending on what you find, you may be able to get by with just a little touch-up and cleaning. Identifying an old finish can suggest the age of a potential project as well (see next page).

To identify a finish, begin by looking for visual clues, like crazing or alligatoring (see next page, step 1). If you are still unsure of the finish material based on visual inspection, try dabbing the finish with various solvents. For example, if denatured alcohol dissolves the old topcoat, the chances are good that it is shellac. And once you know it is shellac, you also know that you have the option of blending out surface problems with a mixture of alcohol and shellac (page 124).

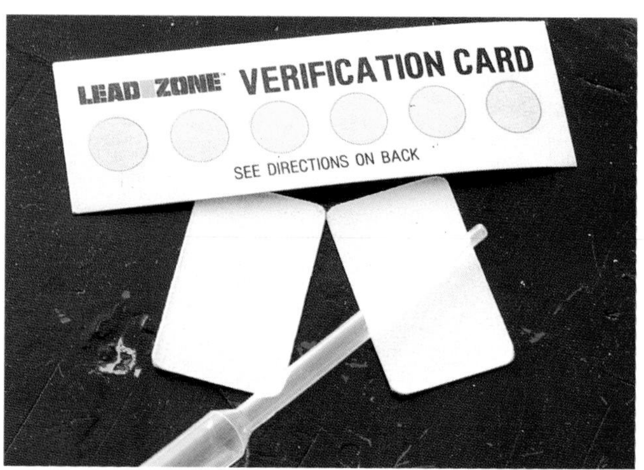

Use a lead-testing kit to determine if a painted finish contains lead. A closely regulated health hazard, lead can be found in paint made before the mid-70s, and was common in paint made before 1950. Follow the kit manufacturer's directions carefully, making sure you test all layers of finish, not just the top layer. If lead is found, do not attempt to strip the paint yourself. Take it to a professional refinisher.

How to Identify an Old Finish

Oil finish:
- has a natural look, often with a flat sheen, but can be polished to high gloss
- frequently tinted with stain that penetrates deep into the wood
- mineral spirits will dissolve oil, but color must be sanded out
- easy to touch up or recoat

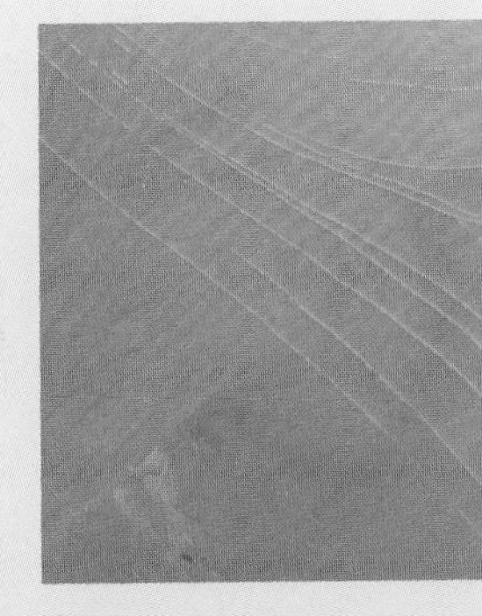

Lacquer:
- very hard finish with a reflective quality; often sprayed on; common on production finishes
- brittle; will craze or fracture (left), especially when exposed to extreme cold
- chips easily
- dissolves and rehardens if treated with lacquer thinner

Shellac:
- alligators and turns dark and gummy as it ages (left)
- usually has an orange cast when dissolved
- very common before 1930, but still in use today
- dissolves easily with denatured alcohol
- will bond with fresh shellac to form a solid topcoat

Varnish/polyurethane:
- most newer varnish products contain polyurethane and are fully dissolved only by strong chemical strippers
- often yellows with age (left)
- common on refinished wood
- polyurethane products cannot be recoated or repaired, but pure varnish may be recoated

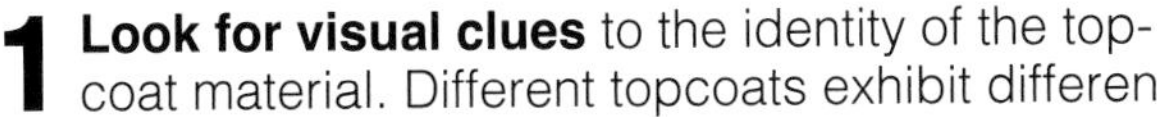

1 **Look for visual clues** to the identity of the topcoat material. Different topcoats exhibit different properties as they age and are subjected to wear and exposure to air and chemicals.

Mineral spirits:
- dissolves wax, most oil topcoats, and pure varnish
- good as a general cleaner
- will lighten some oil-based wood stains

Lacquer thinner:
- dissolves spray-on and brush-on lacquer topcoats
- can be used to repair a lacquer finish (page 124)
- also dissolves shellac and wax
- a more volatile solvent than mineral spirits or alcohol

Denatured alcohol:
- dissolves shellac on contact
- evaporates quickly; must be wiped off soon after application when used as a finish solvent
- also effective on wax and as a general cleaner

Chemical stripper:
- the most powerful finish-removal agent; cuts through varnish and polyurethane
- different brands are made for different finish materials—check the label
- hazardous chemical; use with care (pages 30 to 33)

2 **Test with solvents** to confirm the identity of the finish. If visual inspection has not given you any clues, test the finish working from the mildest solvent to the strongest: mineral spirits, then denatured alcohol, then lacquer thinner, then chemical stripper. To test, dab a little solvent onto a clean rag, then rub the rag on the finish, preferably in an inconspicuous area. Allow time for the solvent to work, then rub again, checking to see if any finish residue comes up on the rag. If none of the solvents dissolve the finish, it is probably a commercial topcoat, and sanding is the only effective removal method.

Selecting a New Finish

A good finish both protects and beautifies wood. To achieve both goals, a finish is made up of several layers, each with its own specific purpose. Each element of a finish should be chosen carefully, according to the features of the wood, the function of the project piece, and your tastes.

On new wood, apply a seal coat made of sanding sealer to create more even finish absorption and more consistent color (page 53). For a fine finish, some woods are best treated with grain filler instead of sealer (page 57).

The next layer is the color layer, which is usually created with wood stain or penetrating oil (pages 58 to 63). Color can either enhance or minimize grain pattern and other wood features, and it can beautify plain wood. With fine woods, or to create a more rustic look, the color layer can be omitted. Dampen the wood surface with mineral spirits to see how it will look with a clear finish. To create a specific decorative look, or to cover wood defects, apply paint as the color layer (pages 64 to 69).

Finally, a topcoat is applied to seal the wood and protect the finished surface from scratches and wear. Topcoats can be created with traditional finishing products, like tung oil, or more contemporary materials, like polyurethane (pages 70 to 79). A layer or two of well-buffed paste wax can be applied over most topcoat materials to create a glossy, protective surface that is easily renewable with fresh wax.

When selecting a new finish, it helps if you know the wood species of your project. Softwoods, like pine, should always be treated with sanding sealer or primer, for example. And open-grained hardwoods, like red oak or mahogany, look better when treated with grain filler. The finish samples on pages 26 to 27 can help you identify the wood type. They also show how some common finishes look on different woods.

As a general rule, base your finish selection on color. Simply choose a color you like, then select a coloring agent and a compatible topcoat.

Consider use, as well. If the finished piece will be used by children or as a food preparation surface, use nontoxic water-based products to finish the wood. For more information on finishing products, refer to the sections indicated above.

A typical wood finish is composed of three basic layers: the seal coat, the color layer, and the topcoat.

Tips for Selecting a New Finish

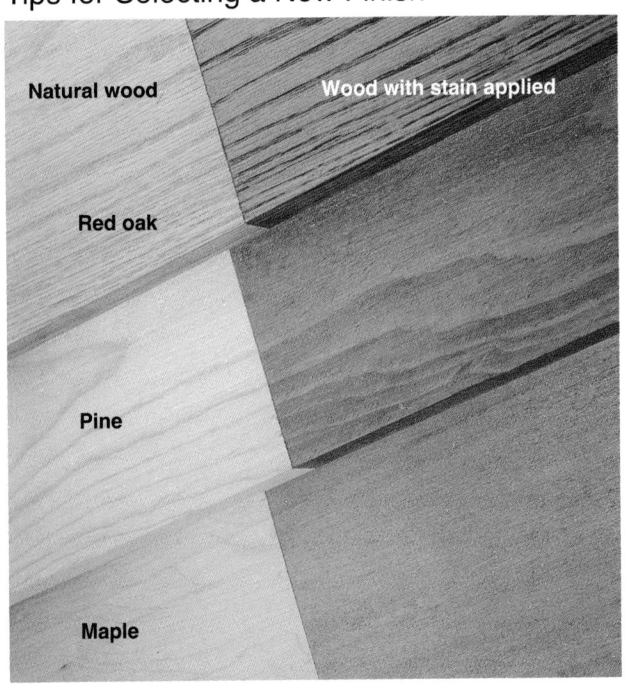

Consider absorption rates. Some wood types absorb more finish materials than others, depending on the porosity of the wood grain. In the photo above, the same stain was applied to three different unsealed woods, resulting in three very different levels of darkness. Sealing the wood with sanding sealer or filling the grain minimizes this effect.

Consider the grain pattern when choosing a finish. Highly figured wood, like the walnut shown above, usually is given a clear finish so the grain is not obscured. In some cases, however, tinted penetrating oil can be used to enhance an already striking grain pattern. Experiment with different coloring agents on a piece of similar wood, or in an inconspicuous area of the project, to help with the finish selection.

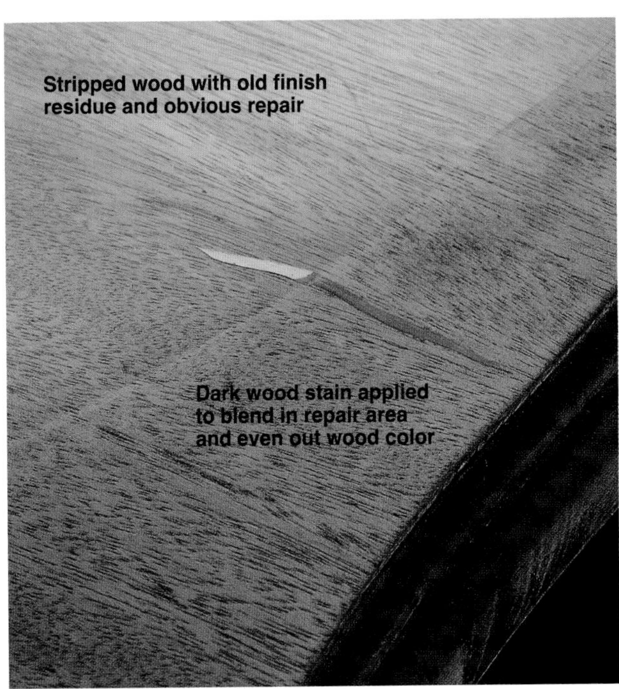

Look for repairs, damage, and uneven color. Workpieces with obvious damage or repairs, like the wood putty line shown above, or with uneven wood color from old finish residue, require a darker finish to disguise the wood defects.

Consider combining colors to create interesting decorative effects. Contrasting stains on the same wood type can create a dramatic finish when used with good design sense.

Sample Finishes: Dark

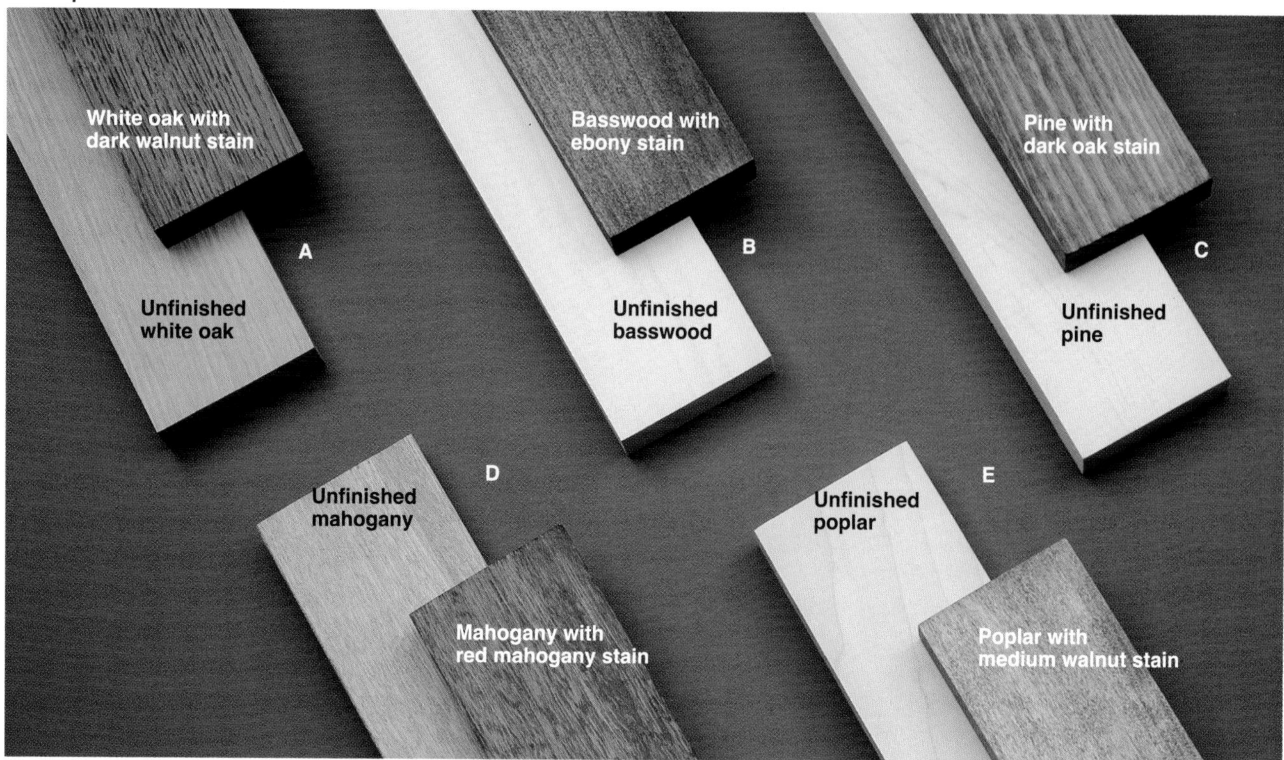

Use dark finishes to: enhance a distinctive grain pattern (A); add interest to plain wood (B); give a rich, formal look to softwoods (C); create a traditional finish style (D); simulate the appearance of a finer hardwood on inexpensive wood (E).

Sample Finishes: Light

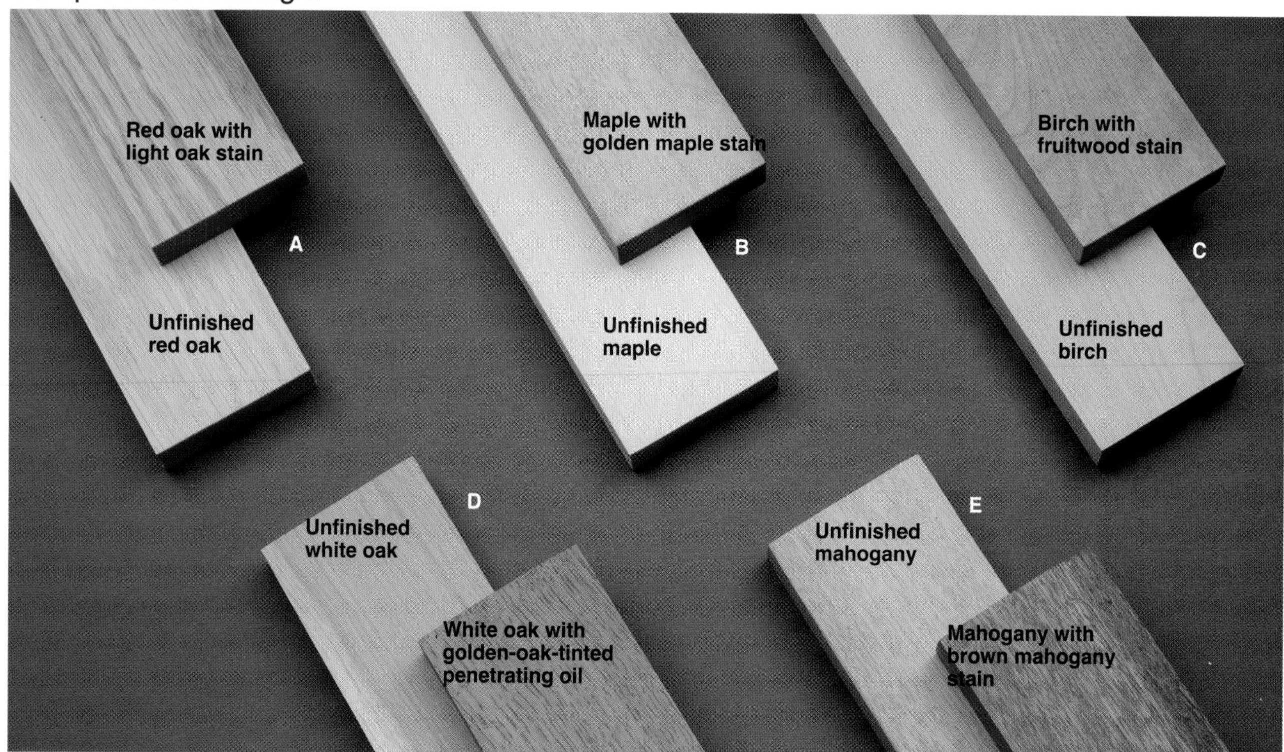

Use light finishes to: highlight subtle grain patterns (A); amplify attractive wood tones (B); modify wood tones to match a particular decor or color scheme (C); add a sense of depth (D); give unfinished wood a seasoned, antique appearance (E).

Sample Finishes: Clear

Clear finishes protect and seal wood while allowing the natural beauty of the wood to speak for itself. Choose clear finishes for exotic woods that are prized for their color or grain pattern, or for more common woods when a natural, rustic look is desired.

Sample Finishes: Painted

Painted finishes mask undesirable qualities, like old finish residue, and create decorative effects. Surface defects, like repairs, stains, knots, and holes should be filled with wood putty to create an even surface when painted. Man-made wood products, like plywood, also benefit from painted finishes.

Power tools for refinishing and finishing include: a belt sander for finish removal on large, flat surfaces; a random-orbit sander for all-purpose sanding; a ½" belt sander for hard-to-reach areas; a power drill with a polishing bonnet for buffing topcoats; a heat gun; and finishing sanders for early stages of finish sanding.

Tools for Refinishing

For any refinishing project, you will need a few hand tools and power tools to remove old finish, repair defects and damage, prepare the workpiece for the new finish, and apply the new finish. You probably already own many of the recommended tools, especially the more basic tools (see list at right). Some household items, like nutpicks, old toothbrushes, and cotton swabs, can be useful in refinishing and finishing. Other household items can be fashioned into custom finish-removal tools, like scrapers made from old credit cards that have been cut to fit the contours of a piece of molding.

Common Tools & Materials

Tools:
- Brad pusher
- Clamps
- Craft knife
- Dust mask
- Eye protection
- Hammer
- Nailset
- Razor blade scraper
- Respirator
- Rubber gloves
- Rubber mallet
- Screwdrivers
- Staple gun
- Straightedge
- Tape measure
- Utility knife
- Wood chisels

Materials:
- Drop cloths
- Masking tape

Brushes for removing finish include: a stripping brush and wire brush for finish removal, and wire detail brushes for smaller areas. **Brushes for applying finish** include: a painting pad for large, flat areas; a polyester-bristle brush for all finishes; a natural-bristle brush for oil-based applications; artists' brushes for detail painting and touch-ups; and stenciling brushes for stenciling, finishing and liquid wax applications.

Sanding and scraping tools include: a stripping tool, paint scraper, and putty knives for finish removal and scraping flat surfaces; detail scrapers for scraping detail areas; a sanding block for all flat surfaces; abrasive pads for finish removal, sanding, and buffing finishing coats; and sanding cord, sanding grips, and a teardrop sanding pad for sanding hard-to-reach areas and contours.

Safety, Cleanup & Disposal

Install fans in windows in your work area to provide ventilation. Where possible, direct one fan outside to remove vapors, and direct another fan into the room to supply fresh air.

Protect yourself and your home, and help ensure good finishing results by using sensible safety, cleanup, and disposal methods when refinishing.

Refinishing wood can create many hazards, including dangerous vapors, flammable or toxic chemical residue, and sanding dust that can impair breathing (as well as ruin an otherwise good finish).

Make sure you have the required safety and protective equipment before you begin working (next page). Establish a dedicated work area, preferably in a well-ventilated area, like a garage. Organize the area for comfort, safety, and efficiency (see guidelines, left). If you are unsure about any disposal regulations, contact your local waste management department, city office, or the Environmental Protection Agency (page 32).

Guidelines for a Refinishing Work Area

- Choose a worksurface that raises the project to a comfortable working height. An adjustable-height workbench is ideal for refinishing.
- Store refinishing knives, scrapers, and other dangerous tools in a locked cabinet or trunk.
- Store hazardous or flammable materials in a fireproof cabinet.
- Protect the floor with a drop cloth. For messy jobs, lay old newspaper over the drop cloth for easy cleanup.
- Cover any ductwork in the work area to keep dust and fumes from spreading throughout the house.
- Extinguish nearby pilot lights and do not operate space heaters whenever working with strippers and other chemicals that produce flammable vapors.
- Maintain a work area that is well lit, dry, and warm (between 65° and 75°F). Use a dehumidifier in damp areas to speed drying times.
- Use a metal trash can with a lid and empty it regularly.

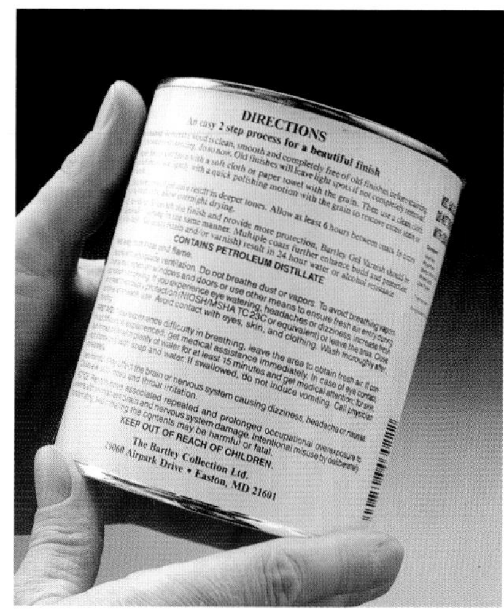

Read product labels for important information on safety, cleanup, and disposal.

Safety Equipment for the Work Area

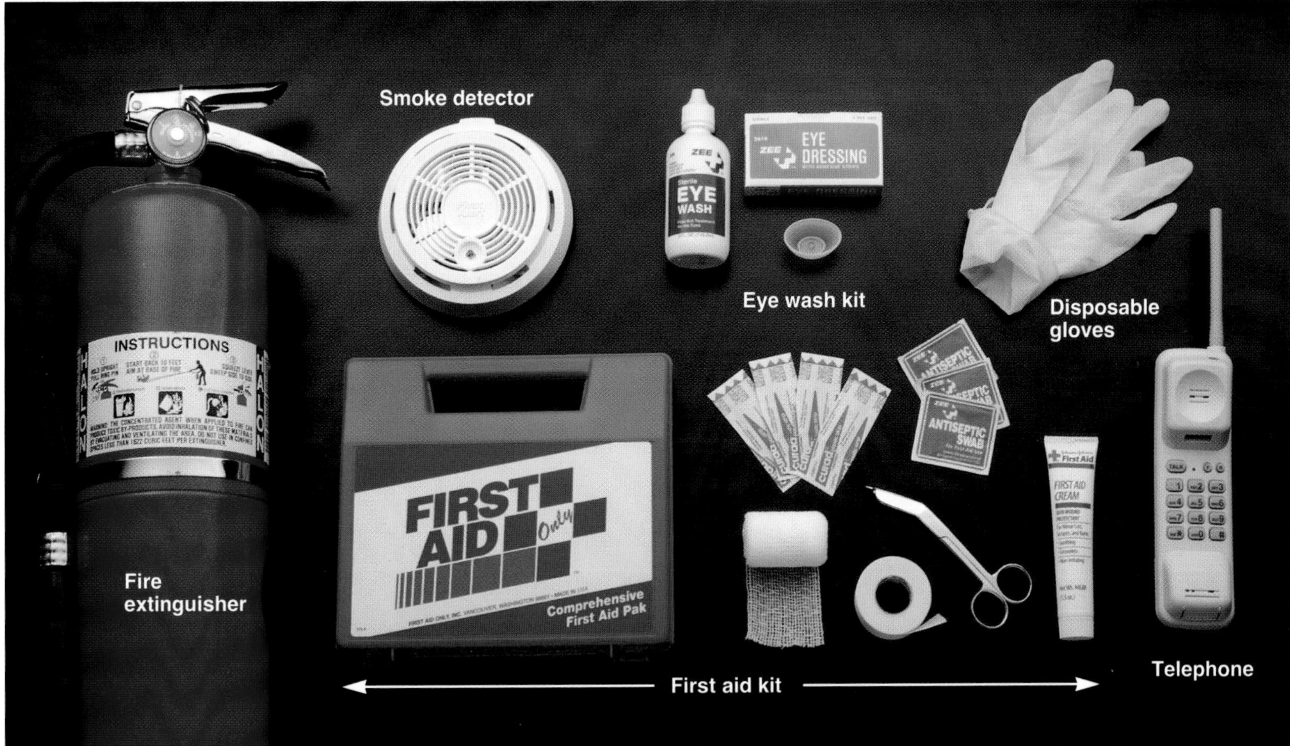

Basic safety equipment for the work area includes: a fully charged fire extinguisher rated for type A and B fires, a smoke detector, a first aid kit, an eye wash kit, disposable latex gloves, and a telephone for emergency use.

Protective Equipment

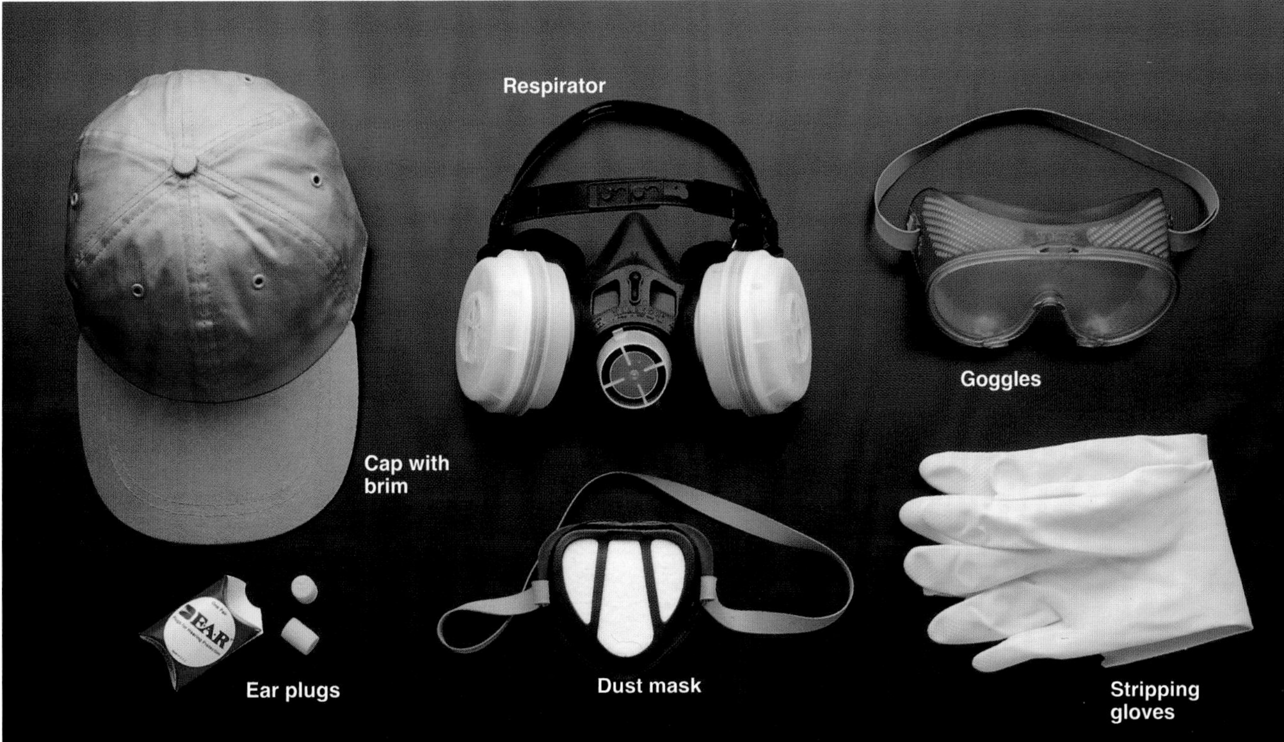

Protective equipment for refinishing and cleanup includes: a dust mask and cap with brim, to wear when sanding; a respirator, to wear when using harsh stripping chemicals; goggles and stripping gloves, to wear while stripping and finishing; ear plugs, to wear when operating power tools.

Storage Tips

Hang paint brushes with the bristles down so they dry evenly and completely, and to protect the bristles. If the bristles are bent while the brush is drying, they will become permanently bent.

Label storage containers clearly with a description of the contents and the date the material was first used. Also note any special projects to which a finishing product was applied. NOTE: The best solution to storage issues is to buy only as much material as you need, avoiding leftovers.

Disposal Tip

Use newspapers and rags to collect residue from refinishing and finishing. Let the newspapers and rags dry, then throw them out with your household trash. NOTE: Any residue containing lead (page 22) must be taken to a hazardous waste disposal site.

Guidelines for Working with Chemicals

Leftover paints, strippers, and solvents are considered household hazardous wastes. Wastes produced by stripping and finishing procedures may contain lead, mercury, and other dangerous substances that will pollute landfills and water supplies. Call the EPA Hazardous Waste Hotline at 1-800-424-9346 for information on disposing of these materials responsibly.

- Use water-based strippers, stains, and finishes instead of oil-based products whenever they meet your needs.
- Buy refinishing and finishing materials in the smallest quantity needed for the job, and dispose of leftover materials properly.
- Never pour refinishing or finishing chemicals down the drain.
- At the end of your project, take any unused chemicals to a hazardous waste disposal site, or donate any usable leftover materials to friends or civic organizations.
- Never mix chemicals directly into your household or yard waste without drying first (see *Tip*, left).

Cleanup Tips

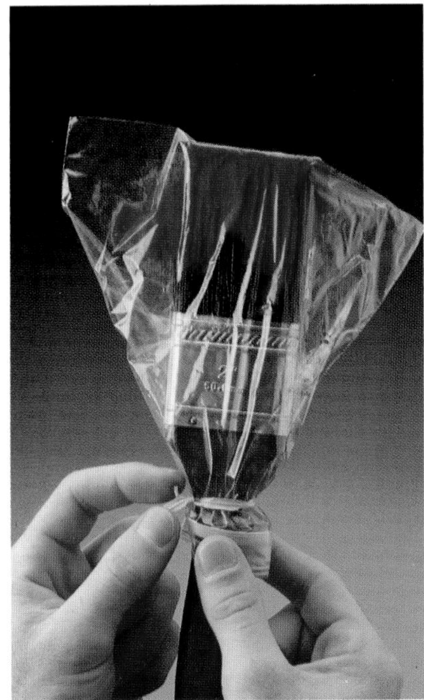

Wrap wet paint brushes in plastic or foil to store them for up to three or four hours while you wait for a coat of finish to dry.

Reuse mineral spirits. Pour used mineral spirits into a clear container, and allow it to rest until the contaminants settle to the bottom of the container. Pour or siphon the clear mineral spirits into another container for later use. Dispose of the residue properly.

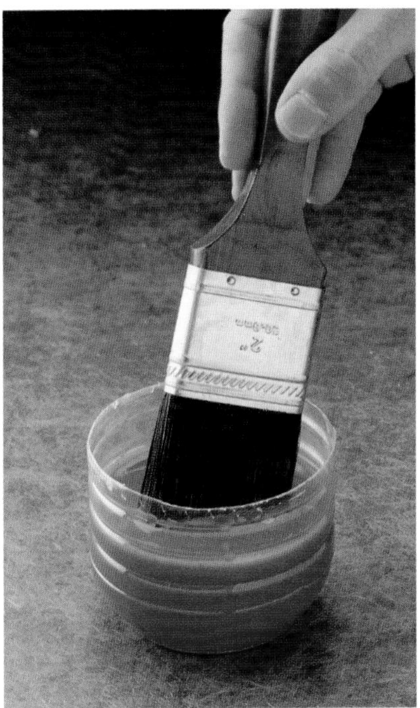

Clean brushes efficiently in a container that is just big enough to hold both the brush and enough solvent to do the job. To ensure compatibility with the solvent, select a container that is made of the same material (usually plastic or metal) as the solvent container.

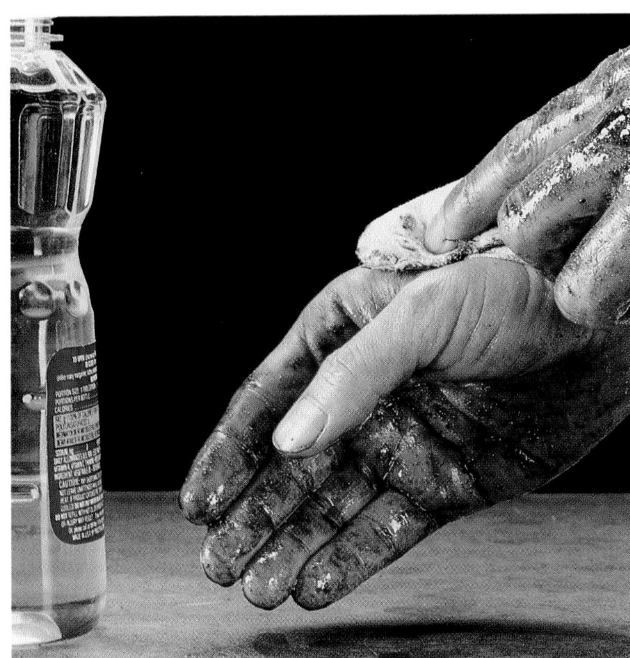

Clean hands with vegetable oil. Scrubbing with ordinary vegetable oil will dissolve and remove most oil-based finishing products. The oily mess it creates is rinsed off easily with soap and water (dish detergent is very effective).

Keep your work area dust free by vacuuming toolboxes, cabinets, woodwork, and light fixtures, as well as all floors and worksurfaces, whenever you complete a sanding project.

Refinishing Basics

Choose the best finish-removal method for the type of finish on your project. On painted surfaces, heat stripping with a heat gun and scraper removes most of the old paint quickly and effectively, leaving only a small amount of residue to be chemically stripped or sanded off.

Removing Old Finishes

Removing an old finish does not have to be a tedious chore. In fact, watching your project emerge from beneath many layers of old finish is one of the most satisfying stages of the refinishing process. Nevertheless, stripping a finish should be viewed as a last resort to be done only if the old finish cannot be saved.

Before beginning the removal process, make certain your project really needs stripping. Clean the wood surfaces thoroughly with mineral spirits and identify the finish topcoat to determine if it can be repaired (pages 22 to 23).

There are three primary finish-removal methods: scraping and sanding, heat stripping, and chemical stripping. Removing finish usually requires a combination of techniques. Scraping and sanding are done at the beginning and end of almost every finish-removal process. Sanding is the only way to remove some very stubborn finishes, like epoxy paint. Heat stripping is most effective with painted finishes, but it can be used with some success on thick layers of clear topcoat. In most cases, heat stripping should be followed by chemical stripping to fully remove a finish.

Chemical stripping is the most thorough finish-removal method. It removes nearly any finish, and it is the only effective removal method for polyurethane products.

This section shows:

- Scraping & Sanding (pages 38 to 39)
- Heat Stripping (pages 40 to 41)
- Chemical Stripping (pages 42 to 43)

Tips for Removing a Finish: Preparing the Workpiece

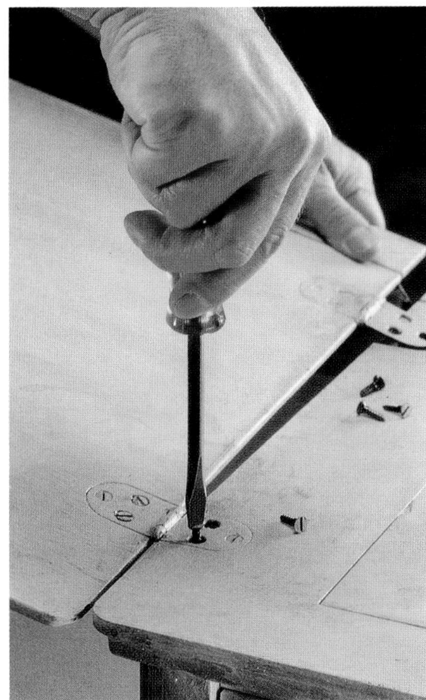

Remove the hardware to provide better access to wood surfaces. Removing the hardware also lets you refurbish it without damaging the wood (pages 80 to 82).

Make repairs to the workpiece (pages 46 to 51). Problems like loose veneer need to be corrected before chemical strippers are applied because the chemicals can get into the damaged area and worsen the problem.

Disassemble furniture when it is helpful (page 47). Some furniture is easier to work with when it is broken down into separate, more accessible pieces.

Mask delicate parts and accessories that are difficult to remove. Especially on older items, trying to remove delicate parts that are securely in place can damage the parts and the wood surrounding them (page 82).

Label all woodwork before sending it out to be commercially stripped. Use a scratch-awl for marking—pen or pencil marks usually disappear during commercial stripping. Make a complete list of the items you send out, and always check your list at pickup time to make sure nothing is missing.

Remove epoxy paint and tough commercial finishes with a belt sander—some commercial finishes, especially those applied to prefinished flooring products, are almost impossible to dissolve with chemicals.

Scraping & Sanding

Abrasion techniques, like scraping and sanding, are used at the start and the end of most finish-removal projects. Before heat stripping or chemically stripping wood, scrape off loose finish with a paint scraper or putty knife. After stripping as much finish as you can, use scrapers again to dislodge any last flecks of finish. Finally, sand to get rid of finish residue and to smooth the wood surface.

Use scraping and sanding as your primary finish-removal method on extra-tough surfaces like epoxy paint (photo, above), and for very delicate surfaces that cannot be heat-stripped or chemically stripped. Sanding is the most common method for removing finish from floors. Use coarse sandpaper (up to 120-grit) for finish removal.

Scrapers and sanding blocks come in all shapes and sizes (page 29). And if the perfect tool for your needs is not manufactured, you can often make it yourself from simple household items, like an old credit card, a rubber spatula, or metal flashing.

NOTE: Sanding to remove a finish is a very different process from finish sanding. For finish-sanding techniques, see pages 52 to 59.

Rent floor sanders for resurfacing wood floors. Drum sanders and edgers like the ones shown above are available at many rental stores. If you rent these tools, make sure to get operating instructions from the attendant, as well as plenty of sanding belts and discs in a variety of grits (you can always return what you do not use). For a demonstration of floor resurfacing, see pages 118 to 121.

Tools for Scraping & Sanding

Paint scrapers remove loosened finish materials. Use a detail scraper with interchangeable scraping heads (left) to remove paint from hard-to-reach spots, and a paint scraper with replaceable blades (right) to scrape flat surfaces.

A belt sander is used for fast finish removal from large, flat surfaces. This tool removes material very quickly, so use it with discretion. Do not hold the belt sander still in one spot—keep it moving constantly or you will create grooves in the surface. NOTE: Never use a belt sander on antiques or fine furniture.

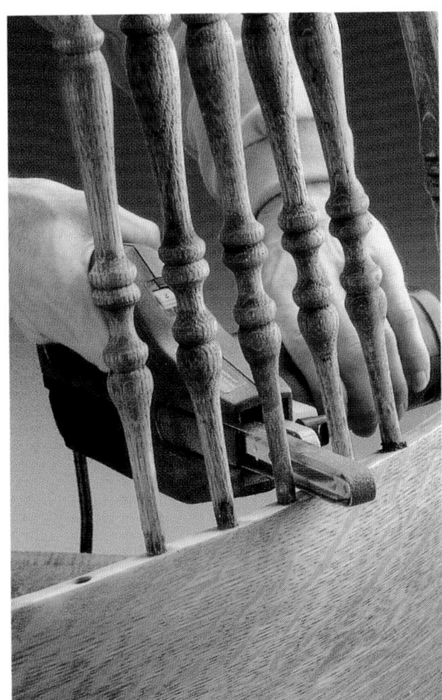

A loop sander is a special-purpose belt sander with a ½"-wide belt. Use this tool to power-sand a finish in hard-to-reach spots.

Sanding cords remove finish from crevices, like those commonly found on spindles and decorative accents. Cords are sold in several different grits: 60- to 120-grit cord is good for finish removal.

Teardrop sanding blocks in a variety of sizes let you sand old finish from contours or unusually shaped areas. They can also be used for finish sanding. Similar products, called sanding grips, are available in many shapes and sizes (page 29).

Successful heat stripping depends on good timing. As you expose paint to a heat gun, the paint reaches a point where its bond with the wood loosens. If you scrape the surface at this point, the scraper works like a plow, pushing the loosened paint off the wood in wide ribbons. If you wait too long, the paint becomes gummy.

Heat Stripping

Heat stripping is a safe and effective finish-removal method when the proper techniques and safety measures are used. It works best on paint, but can be used on thick layers of varnish, lacquer, and other topcoats. Heat stripping is a good money-saver when done prior to chemical stripping: because it removes so much old paint, you will use less of the expensive chemical stripper. Use caution when heat stripping woodwork—the blower can send hot paint chips flying, so always scrape off loose paint before using the heat gun.

Everything You Need:

Tools: heat gun, putty knife, assorted scrapers, heavy-gauge extension cord, fire extinguisher.

Materials: coffee can, goggles, work gloves, aluminum foil and cardboard.

Tip for Heat Stripping

A heat shield prevents the hot air from a heat gun from damaging or blistering other areas next to the work area. To make a heat shield, cover a piece of heavy cardboard (approximately 6" × 12") with heavy-duty aluminum foil.

How to Heat-strip Paint

1 Scrape off all loose paint flakes with a paint scraper. Position the heat gun about 2" above a large, flat surface, then turn the gun on, starting at the lowest setting. As the gun heats up, move it in a circular motion until the paint begins to release—usually signified by blistering. If the paint fails to blister, try the next higher heat setting.

2 Push a metal scraper along the heated surface, at an angle of approximately 30°, following the heat gun. Develop a rhythm that allows you to move the scraper and the heat gun at the same speed (always keep the heat gun moving in a circular motion). Strip all the large, flat surfaces. TIP: Keep the scraper blade clean by depositing paint ribbons into a coffee can as you work.

3 Heat-strip the contoured and uneven areas, using specialty scrapers, where needed, to remove the loosened paint. Do not overheat or apply too much pressure around detailed areas—they are more vulnerable to scorching and gouging than flat areas.

4 Dry-scrape all wood surfaces to remove any remaining loosened paint flecks after you are done heat stripping. In most cases, you will need to use chemical solvents or strippers to remove the rest of the finish (see next page).

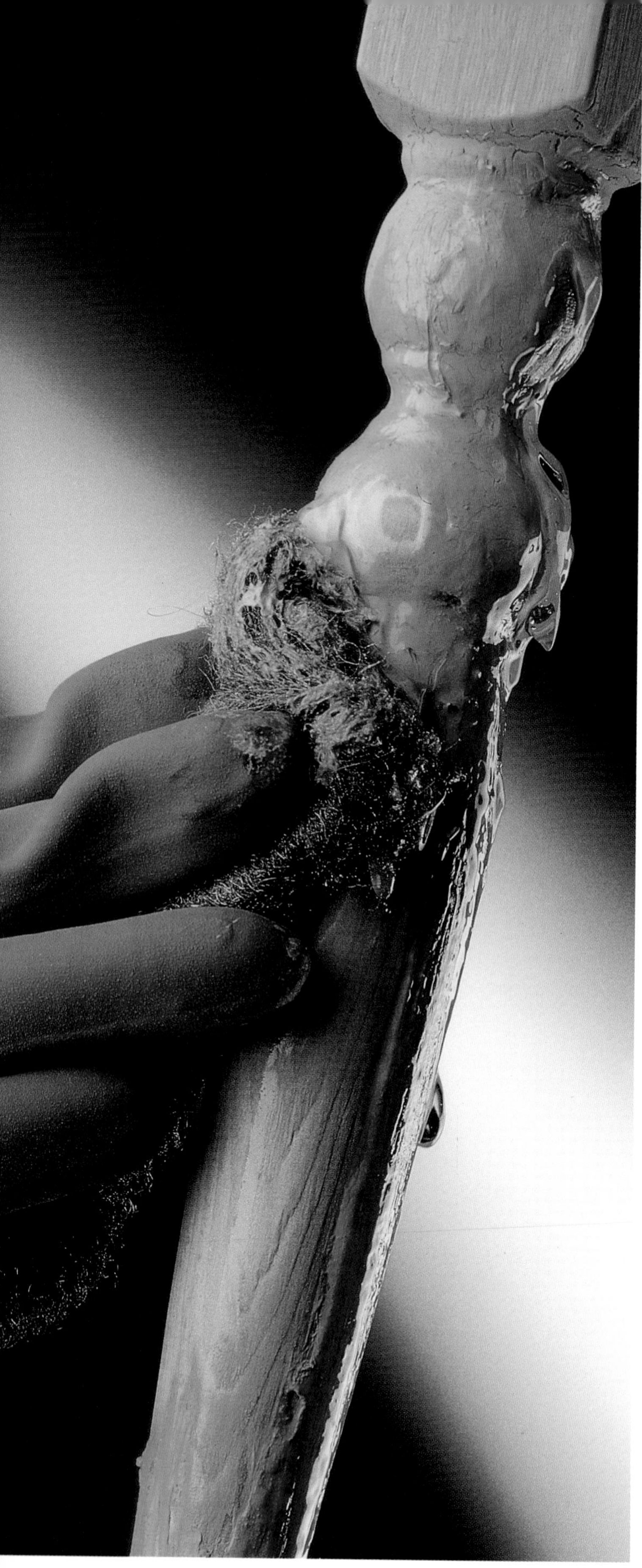

Chemical stripper dissolves thick finishes so they can be wiped off or scraped off easily. Coarse abrasive pads are effective removal tools for contours.

Chemical Stripping

Dissolving an old finish with chemical solvents is a fast and thorough removal technique. Use chemicals to help remove just about any finish material, from varnish to polyurethane to paint.

Before you choose a chemical solvent or stripper for your refinishing project, identify the old finish type (pages 22 to 23). Keep in mind that most finishes are composed of several different materials, and try to select a chemical that is effective on all of these materials.

The primary solvents used to strip a finish are: mineral spirits (used as a general cleaner, for removing wax buildup, and to dissolve pure varnish); denatured alcohol (effective on shellac and as a rinsing agent after stripping); and lacquer thinner (used to dissolve both spray-on and brush-on lacquer finishes). These chemicals are inexpensive and relatively safe to use, so use them instead of commercial chemical strippers whenever you can.

Commercial finish strippers are strong chemicals that dissolve just about any finish. For most jobs, semi-paste stripper is the best choice. Unlike liquid stripper, it clings to any surface and will not dry out before the finish is dissolved. There is quite a range of semi-paste strippers to choose from. By reading the labels, you will find that most are created for specific finish types. There are varnish removers, paint removers, and even polyurethane removers.

In the past, strippers almost always contained hazardous chemicals, requiring you to wear a respirator and other protective equipment. These types are still common, and they are very effective. But for most refinishing jobs, friendlier strippers are a better choice. New products without hazardous chemicals will dissolve most finishes with far less risk, although they are often a little slower. See pages 30 to 32 for information on storing and disposing of strippers and solvents.

Everything You Need:

Tools: paint brushes, putty knives and scrapers, safety equipment.

Materials: stripper or solvent, medium abrasive pads, newspapers and rags, sawdust, rinsing agent.

How to Chemically Strip a Finish

1 Transfer some stripper (but not more than you can use in 15 minutes) to a smaller, easy-to-use container. Select a brush for applying the stripper—most brands may be applied with inexpensive polyester-bristle brushes.

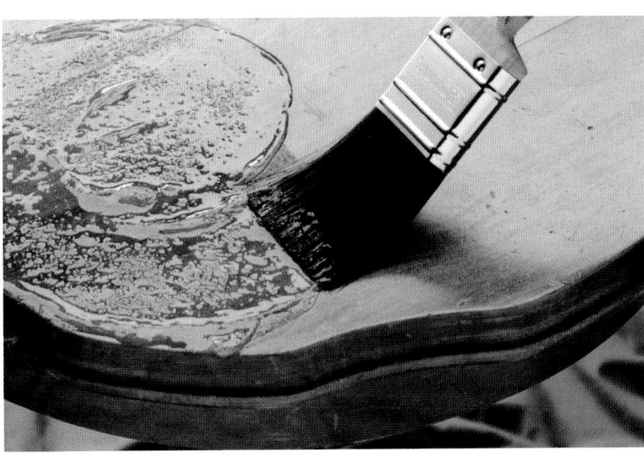

2 Wearing gloves and a respirator, apply a thick coat of stripper (1/8" to 1/4") to the workpiece, beginning with any large, flat surfaces at the top of the project, and working down from there. Do not overbrush the stripper.

3 Let the stripper work for at least 30 minutes (see manufacturer's directions). TIP: Sprinkle sawdust on the stripper to make it easier to remove. Remove the sludge with a putty knife or stripping knife, and deposit it on old newspapers (pages 30 to 32).

4 Strip the detailed and contoured areas, using specialty scrapers and abrasive pads to remove the sludge (page 29). Use light pressure on the scrapers so you do not gouge the wood.

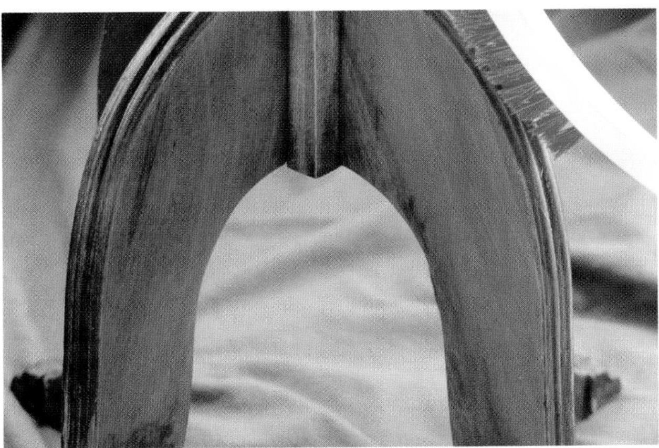

5 Apply a thin coat of stripper to the stripped wood surfaces, then scrub off any remaining finish, using a synthetic-bristle stripping brush or medium abrasive pads.

6 Clean the wood with a medium abrasive pad dipped in the rinsing agent recommended by the stripper manufacturer (often denatured alcohol). This removes most traces of the finish and the stripper.

Making repairs, like regluing the face-frame stretcher joints on this dresser, helps ensure that your project piece will stand up to daily use for many years to come.

Making Basic Repairs

Repair broken parts, loose joints, damaged veneer, and other wood problems during the refinishing process. By making careful repairs, you will be able to enjoy your completed refinishing project for a long time.

This section shows you how to make basic repairs to common problems found in all types of furniture, floors, and woodwork. Most repairs involve wood joints. If you are unfamiliar with the various ways two pieces of wood can be joined together, check libraries and bookstores for information on wood joinery.

Once you identify any repairs your refinishing project requires, choose the best time to perform the repairs. Some repairs, like reattaching loose veneer, should almost always be done before chemical stripping because the chemicals can seep under loose veneer and cause further damage. Other repairs, like regluing a broken joint, make more sense after the stripping is completed because chemical strippers can dissolve the new glue in the joint.

To learn more about cosmetic repairs, like filling scratches in a finish or reattaching wood splinters, see *Maintenance & Quick Fixes* (pages 122 to 125).

This section shows:

- Repairing Joints & Broken Parts (pages 46 to 49)
- Repairing Veneer (pages 50 to 51)

Glues & Gluing Tools

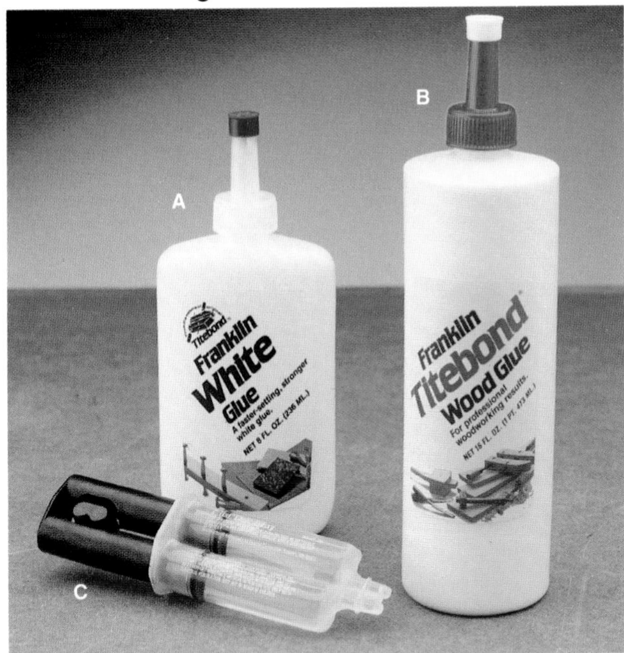

Common glues for repairing wood include: white glue (A), carpenter's glue (B), and epoxy glue (C). Carpenter's glue is suitable for most general wood repairs, but for complicated repairs use slower-drying white glue to give yourself more working time. Use epoxy for exterior furniture and for repairs where the glue must fill voids created by missing wood.

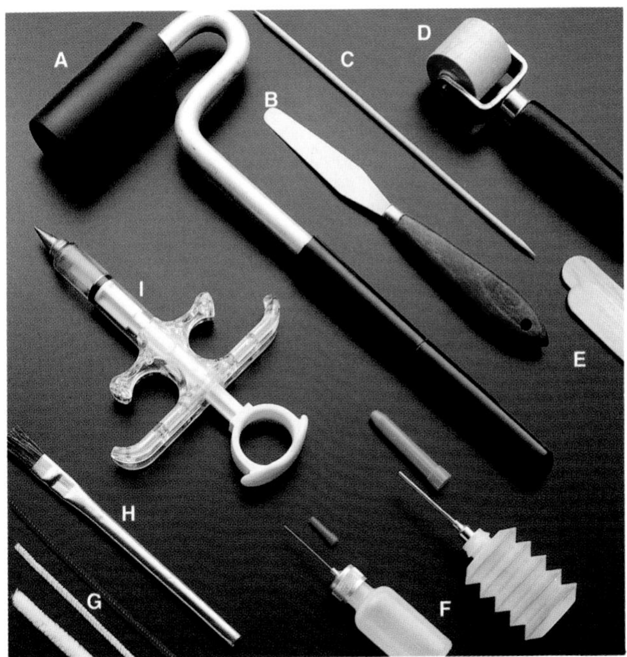

Tools for gluing include: a J-roller (A), and a wood wallpaper seam roller (D) for pressing veneer; and glue applicators, like a palette knife (B), a skewer (C), tongue depressors or popsicle sticks (E), squeeze bottles (F), pipe cleaners (G), a metal glue brush (H), and a glue injector (I).

Tips for Working with Glue

Remove old glue before regluing. Use a file or an emery board in tight areas, and use scrapers or chisels on flat, easy-to-reach surfaces. Stubborn glue can usually be dissolved with hot vinegar.

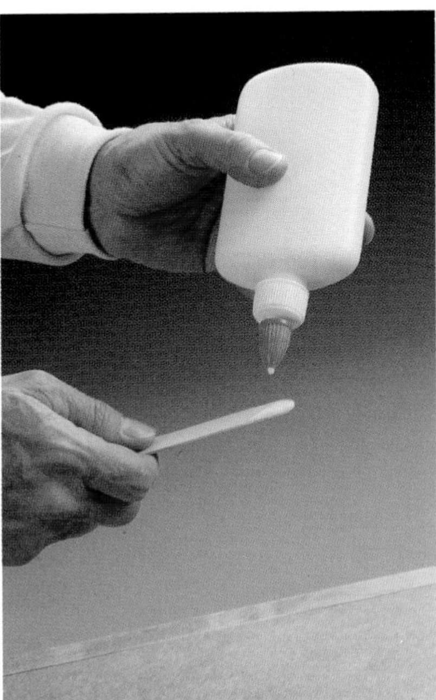

Apply glue to the applicator, not to the workpiece itself, to achieve the neatest results when gluing in hard-to-reach areas, like under veneer or inside a mortise.

Scrape off excess glue after it dries, using a chisel (round over the corners first to prevent gouging). Wiping off wet glue with a rag forces glue into wood pores, interfering with new finish absorption.

Repairing Joints & Broken Parts

Cut hardwood mending plates and matching mortises to reinforce repairs made to cracks or breaks in flat surfaces (page 48). Cut a bow-tie-shaped plate, and mortise (above) with a chisel. Or, if you prefer working with a router, cut figure-8 shapes (inset).

Loose or broken joints and broken parts, like cracked seats and wobbly legs, are among the most common structural problems found in furniture. Easy to fix, these problems usually can be corrected simply by gluing and reinforcing the joint. For best results, disassemble the joint first so you can scrape off the old glue before regluing. Doing good, careful work is important—if the repair is not as strong as the original joint, it is likely to fail again.

Everything You Need:

Tools: chisel, putty knife, clamps, drill, glue injector, saw, utility knife, nail puller, pliers, bandsaw or jig saw, pencil, screwdriver.

Materials: carpenter's glue, epoxy glue, wood sweller, dowels, wood, wax paper, hardwood wedge.

Tips for Repairing Joints Without Disassembly

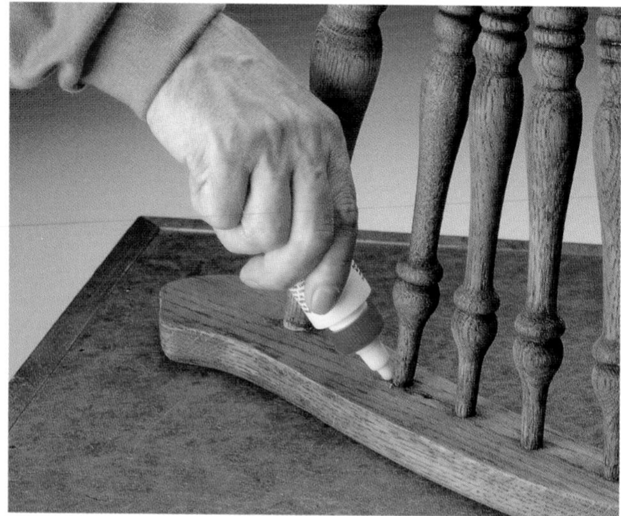

Use wood sweller to tighten loose joints. When squirted into a loose joint, like a chair spindle, sweller causes the wood in the joint to swell and tighten. Use wood swellers only on interior spindles and other parts that do not support much weight when the furniture is in use.

Drill holes in a joint and fill with epoxy glue to create "epoxy nails" that harden and reinforce loose joints. Drill at least two 3/16"-diameter holes per joint. Unlike metal fasteners, epoxy will not corrode or discolor the wood. Use a self-mixing injector (above) to deliver the correct mixture of two-part epoxy glue.

How to Disassemble a Joint

1 Remove nails, screws, and other fasteners that were driven into the wood to reinforce the joint. Internal reinforcement, like dowels or biscuits, cannot be removed until the joint is separated.

2 If the glue bond is still intact, dissolve the glue by injecting hot vinegar into the joint. NOTE: If hot vinegar fails to dissolve the glue, it is probably epoxy, which must be separated by breaking or cutting the joint.

3 Wiggle or twist the joint gently before the glue rehardens. If it still does not separate, drive a wedge-shaped hardwood scrap into the joint.

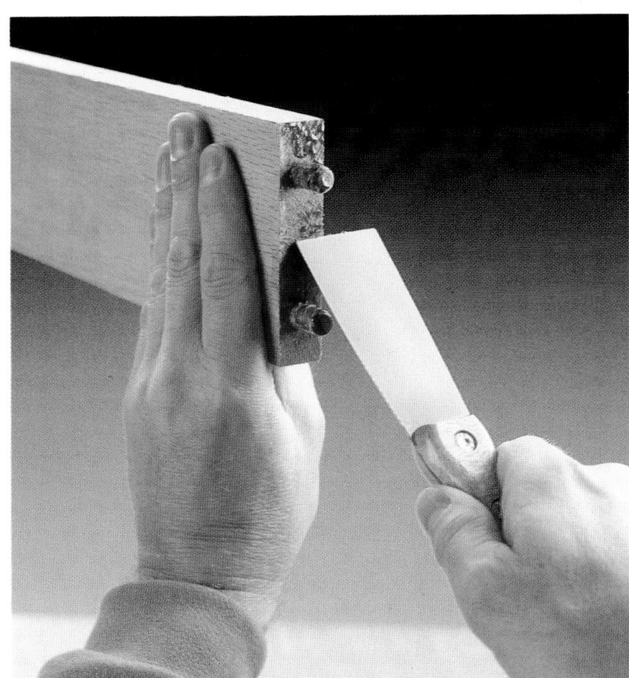

4 Scrape all traces of the old glue from the parts of the joint (including wooden fasteners like dowels or biscuits) using a sharp tool, like a putty knife, chisel, or file.

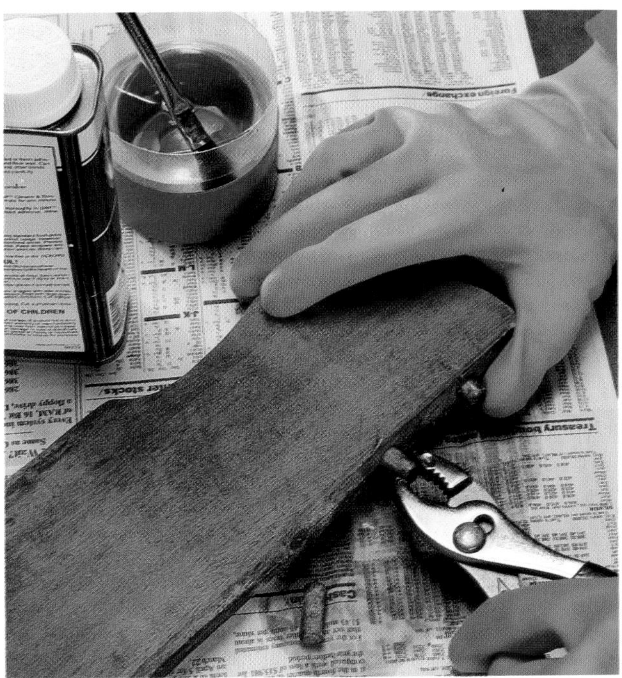

OPTION: Remove internal reinforcement, like dowels—especially if the joint has rotted or deteriorated in any way. Use a pliers to pull dowels or biscuits out of the wood, then replace them with new reinforcing materials.

How to Repair Cracks & Breaks in Flat Surfaces

1 Clean loose debris and splinters from the pieces of the part so the mating surfaces fit tightly. If so much wood is missing that the pieces cannot be matched, you probably need to replace the damaged part.

2 Apply glue to the surfaces to be joined, press the parts together, then clamp the glue joint and let the glue dry. Unclamp, then scrape the excess glue from the surfaces with a chisel.

3 Outline and cut a bow-tie-shaped mending plate from 1/4"-thick hardwood. When set over the crack or break, it should overhang each side of the break by at least 1". Cut the mending plate using a bandsaw or jig saw with a medium or fine blade.

4 Position the mending plate over the crack or break, then trace the outline onto the underside of the workpiece as a guide for cutting the mortise. Use a sharp wood chisel to cut a 3/16"-deep mortise for the mending plate. Smooth out the bottom and sides of the mortise, using the chisel or a file. Test-fit the plate in the mortise, and enlarge the mortise if needed.

5 Apply glue to the back of the mending plate and to the bottom of the mortise, then set the plate into the mortise. Cover the plate with wax paper, then clamp until the glue is dry. Scrape away the excess glue with a chisel, then sand the top of the plate so it is flush with the surrounding wood.

How to Repair Broken Spindles, Legs & Rungs

1 Remove the spindle, leg, or rung from the piece of furniture, disassembling the joints if they are not loose already (page 47). Clean debris and splinters from the pieces of the part so the mating surfaces fit tightly. If so much wood is missing that the pieces cannot be matched, you probably need to replace the damaged part.

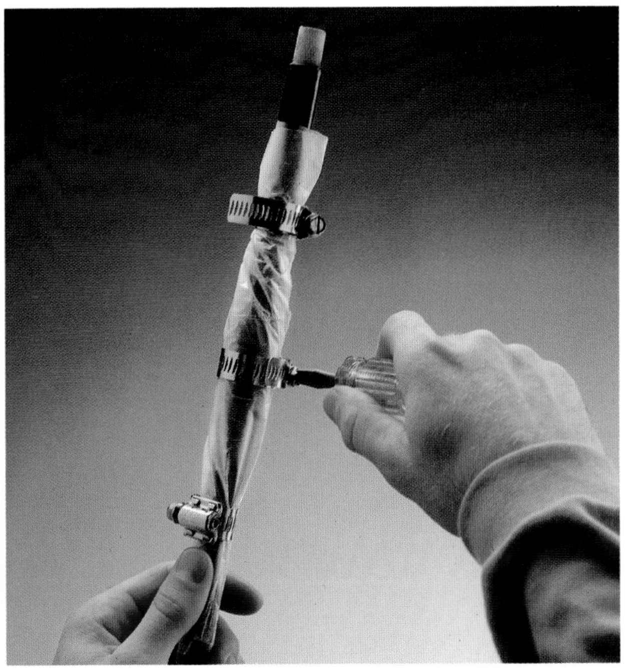

2 Apply glue to the mating surfaces of the break. Wrap the spindle, leg, or rung with wax paper so the clamps do not stick to the wood, then press the parts together, making sure they are aligned. Slip hose clamps over the repair, spaced every 3" to 4", and tighten them securely. Allow the glue to dry overnight, then remove the clamps and paper, and scrape away the excess glue with a chisel.

3 Choose a length of hardwood dowel that is no thicker in diameter than one-half the diameter of the spindle, leg, or rung at the repair spot (the thickest spot in the repair area). Using a drill and a bit the same diameter as the dowel, drill a hole all the way through the thickest spot in the repair area.

4 Taper one end of the dowel (inset photo), then cut the dowel so it is ½" longer than the depth of the hole. Apply glue to the dowel and slide it into the hole, leading with the tapered end, so it extends ¼" on each side of the hole. When the glue is dry, trim the ends of the dowel with a saw or file, then sand them flush.

Use small tools when working with veneer. Thin-blade knives, like the palette knife above, and small brushes are less likely to cause damage.

Repairing Veneer

Making basic veneer repairs, like regluing loose or blistered veneer, is a fairly simple job. As long as you clean the repair area thoroughly and do not rush through the process, these easy veneer repairs will greatly improve the appearance of your furniture—and prevent further damage. Complicated repairs involving patching should be done by a professional.

Before regluing loose veneer, try ironing the veneer to reform the glue bond (page 123).

Everything You Need:

Tools: brush, palette or putty knife, glue applicator, squeeze bottle for glue, craft knife, pencil, straightedge, clamps.

Materials: glue, wax paper, vinegar, cotton swab.

Common Veneer Problems

Loose or blistered veneer is relatively easy to repair. In some cases, the repair is as simple as covering the damaged area with a towel, then pressing it with an iron (page 123). If ironing does not work, reglue the veneer with fresh glue (page opposite). Scratches, burns, and other common surface problems are repaired using the same techniques as with solid wood—but use extra care and do not oversand.

Missing sections of veneer are difficult to repair. If you still have the missing piece and it is intact, however, it can be reglued the same way as with loose veneer (see opposite page). Cutting and gluing down new veneer patches is a job for professionals or very experienced woodworkers. Often, the best solution is to cover the entire surface with new veneer.

How to Repair Loose Veneer

1 Use a putty or palette knife to lift the veneer so you can clean below it with a brush. Be careful not to tear the fragile veneer If there is glue on the surface, try scrubbing with a cotton swab dipped in hot vinegar.

2 Apply glue to the veneer and base with an applicator, like a cotton swab. OPTION: Inject glue under the veneer with a squeeze bottle or a glue injector (page 45).

3 Cover the repair area with wax paper and a clamping block, then clamp the repair until the glue dries. Remove the clamp and carefully scrape away any excess glue with a chisel.

How to Repair Blistered Veneer

1 Slice the blister along the grain with a craft knife. Use a thin-bladed knife, like a palette knife, and a small brush to clean debris from under the blistered area (see opposite page).

2 Slip a thin spacer under the veneer, then inject carpenter's glue into the blister (for very large areas, use slower-drying white glue). Roll the blister with a seam roller (page 45) to set the glue. Cover with wax paper and clamp the repair until the glue dries.

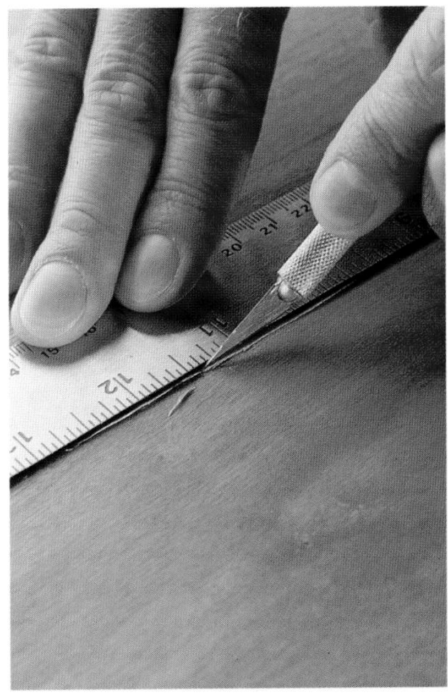

3 Slice away any veneer that overlaps the seam, using a craft knife and straightedge.

Sand wood with power sanders, like the random-orbit sander shown above, to make quick work of the initial finish sanding stages, while producing a very smooth wood surface.

Preparing for the Finish

A properly prepared wood surface absorbs finish materials evenly, focusing attention on the quality and color of the wood and the finish. A poorly prepared surface focuses attention on itself and its flaws.

Sanding or filling scratches and gouges, removing dents and stains, and carefully finish sanding are the essential steps in preparing for the finish. With many woods (especially softwoods like pine) you can create a more even finish by sealing the wood with sanding sealer immediately after finish sanding, then sanding the sealer lightly with 220-grit sandpaper after it dries. For exceptionally smooth, rich finishes (particularly on open-grain hardwoods like mahogany), apply wood grain filler to fill in checks and large pores, creating a smooth-as-glass surface.

Before beginning the final preparations for the finish, sand the workpiece with medium-grit sandpaper to remove small scratches and other surface problems—this is especially important if you did not use sanding as a final stage of finish removal. Any scratches, gouges, dents, or stains that survive the intermediate sanding should be remedied before you finish-sand.

Do your final stage of finish sanding immediately before you apply the finish—the smooth surface created by finish sanding is easily scratched or discolored.

This section shows:

- Fixing Surface Flaws (pages 54 to 55)
- Making Final Surface Preparations (pages 56 to 57)

Tips for Preparing a Wood Surface

Sandpaper Grit Chart

Grit	Task
80 to 100	Finish removal
120 to150	Preliminary finish sanding
180	Final sanding for softwood; intermediate stage of finish sanding for hardwood
220	Final sanding for hardwood
300 to 400	Sanding between finish layers
600 wet/dry	Wet sanding of final finish layer

Choose the right sandpaper for the job. *Aluminum oxide* and *garnet* are two common types. Aluminum oxide is a good general-use product suitable for most refinishing and finishing purposes. Garnet is usually cheaper than aluminum oxide, but it wears out much more quickly. Use sandpaper with the proper grit (higher numbers indicate finer grit—see chart above).

Nonstainable wood putty

Stainable wood putty

Use stainable wood putty to repair scratches and gouges in unfinished wood. Finish materials are not absorbed by nonstainable wood putty, which is usually meant to be used for touch-up after the finish is applied. Read container labels carefully before you purchase wood putty.

Apply wood grain filler that approximately matches the natural color of your wood. Available in light and dark colors, grain filler creates a smooth surface in open wood grains. Usually manufactured as a gel, it can be applied with a putty knife or a rag, but the excess material should be wiped off with a plastic scraper (page 57).

Make your own sanding sealer by blending one part clear topcoat material with one part topcoat solvent. NOTE: Use the same topcoat material you plan to apply to the project. Sanding sealer is used before coloring soft or open-grain woods to achieve even stain penetration. To apply, wipe on a heavy coat, then wipe off the excess after a few minutes. Sand lightly with 220-grit sandpaper when dry.

Fixing Surface Flaws

Before you finish-sand wood, fill scratches, nicks, gouges, and sanded-out burn marks with wood putty. On stripped wood, you may use untinted stainable wood putty, then color it after finish sanding to match the wood color; or you may use pretinted stainable putty that is close in color to the natural wood tone.

Raise shallow dents by swelling the damaged wood with water or steam, and remove or lighten stains with household chlorine bleach or oxalic acid.

Stain untinted wood putty to match the color of the surrounding wood. Wait until after you have finish-sanded the wood to apply the stain. For best results, choose a stain that is the same brand as the wood stain you plan to use on the project. TIP: To find a better stain match, dampen the wood with mineral spirits before comparing it to stain colors.

Everything You Need

Tools: putty knife, paint brushes, pointed scraper, iron, sponge.

Materials: sandpaper, distilled water, oxalic acid crystals, wood putty, bleach, vinegar, clean cloth.

Tips for Fixing Surface Flaws

Swell out shallow dents with water or steam. Apply a few drops of distilled water into the dent (left), and let the water soak in. In most cases, this will cause dented wood to swell to its original shape. If the dent does not swell out, try touching the tip of a hot iron to a wet rag directly over the dent (right). If all else fails, fill the dent with wood putty (page opposite).

Remove black stains created by water damage or contact with metal using a mixture of oxalic acid crystals (sold at most building centers and paint stores) and distilled water.

Tips for Bleaching Wood

Remove spot stains with household chlorine bleach. Working in an area with good ventilation, brush undiluted bleach onto the stain and wait 20 minutes. To help activate the bleach, set the workpiece in direct sunlight. Rinse off bleach with water, and reapply as needed.

Lighten uneven coloration that is caused by stain residue or spot bleaching, using a 1:1 mixture of water and household chlorine bleach. Sponge the mixture over the wood surface, wait 20 minutes, then rinse off bleach with water. Reapply as needed.

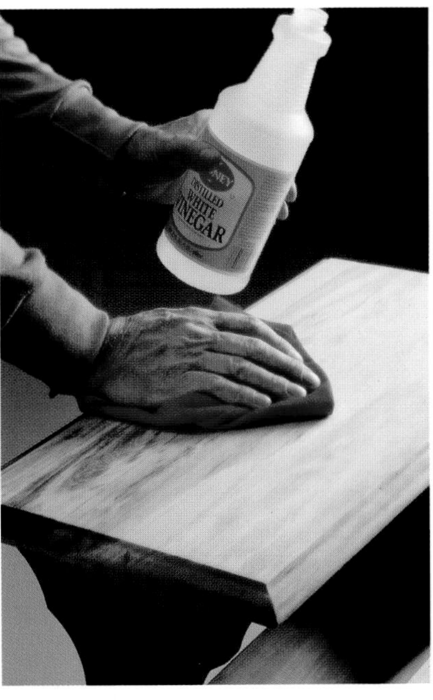

Neutralize bleach with white vinegar. If left in the wood, bleach can cause discoloration and raise wood grain. As soon as you are done bleaching, wipe vinegar onto the bleached area with a rag, then rinse off immediately with water. Dry with a rag.

How to Fill Flaws with Wood Putty

1 Clean out the damaged area with a pointed scraper, like a modeling tool or nutpick, to remove debris that prevents the putty from bonding. If the flaw is very shallow, deepen it with the scraper.

2 Fill the damaged area with stainable wood putty, then scrape away the excess until the putty is just above the surface of the wood. Let the putty dry.

3 Sand the putty so it is level with the wood surface. After finish sanding, color untinted putty with stain or a touch-up marker to match the color and grain pattern of the wood (page 124).

Making Final Surface Preparations

Ensure an even, quality finish by carefully preparing the wood surface. Finish-sand with progressively finer grits of sandpaper, starting with 150-grit. Generally, hardwood requires finer-grit sandpaper than softwood (see chart on page 53). For speed and even results, use a power sander for the first stages of finish sanding. Use hand-sanding with the finest grit in the sequence so you do not oversand.

Seal wood with sanding sealer to create more even finish absorption. Apply grain filler to open-grain hardwood for a deep, smooth finish. Because they decrease stain absorption, sealing and filling create lighter finishes.

Use sanding sealer or grain filler for a fine finish. Finish sanding alone creates a smooth surface, but because wood absorbs stain at different rates, the color can be blotchy and dark. Sealing with sanding sealer (page 53) evens out the stain-absorption rates, yielding a lighter, more even finish. Filling the grain creates a lighter finish that feels as smooth as it looks.

Everything You Need:

Tools: finishing sander, sanding blocks, plastic scraper, work light, wire brush.

Materials: sandpaper, abrasive pads, cloths, sanding sealer or grain filler.

Tips for Finish Sanding

Examine the workpiece with bright sidelighting during finish sanding to gauge your progress. If shadows, scratches, or sanding marks are visible, more sanding is needed.

Wipe the wood surface clean whenever you change sandpaper grits, using a cloth slightly dampened with mineral spirits. This removes dust and grit from coarser sandpaper that cause scratches when you continue sanding.

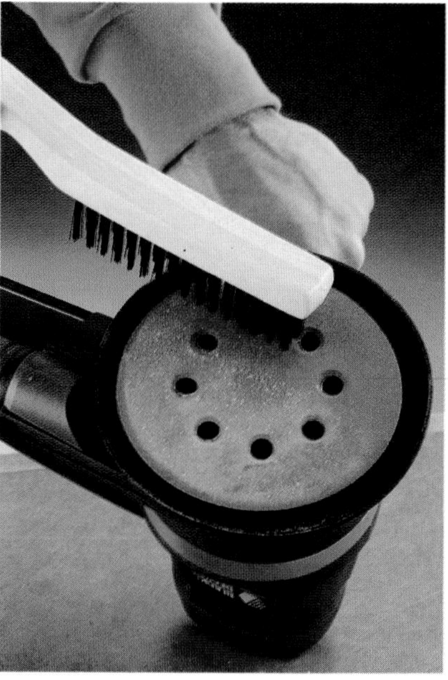

Clean your sandpaper regularly with a wire brush to remove sawdust and grit that can clog the sandpaper and cause burnishing of the wood surface.

How to Finish-sand

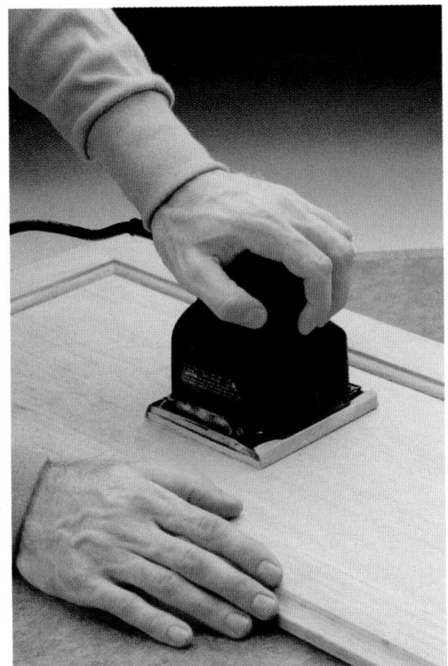

1 Finish-sand all surfaces with 150-grit sandpaper, following the direction of the grain. Use a finishing sander on flat surfaces and specialty sanding blocks on contours. When sanding hardwood, switch to 180-grit paper and sand again (see chart, page 53).

2 Raise the wood grain by dampening the surface with a wet rag. Let the wood dry, then skim the surface with a fine abrasive pad, following the grain. The pad pulls out raised fibers, decreasing the chance of raising the grain during finishing.

3 Use sanding blocks to hand-sand the entire workpiece with the finest-grit paper in the sanding sequence. Sand until all sanding marks are gone and the surface is smooth. If using sanding sealer (page 53), apply a coat now, then sand lightly with 220-grit when dry.

How to Apply Grain Filler

1 After finish sanding, use a rag or putty knife to spread a coat of grain filler (page 53) onto the wood surface. With a polishing motion, work the filler into the grain. Let the filler dry until it becomes cloudy (usually about five minutes).

2 Remove excess filler by drawing a plastic putty scraper across the grain of the wood at a 45° angle. Let the grain filler dry overnight.

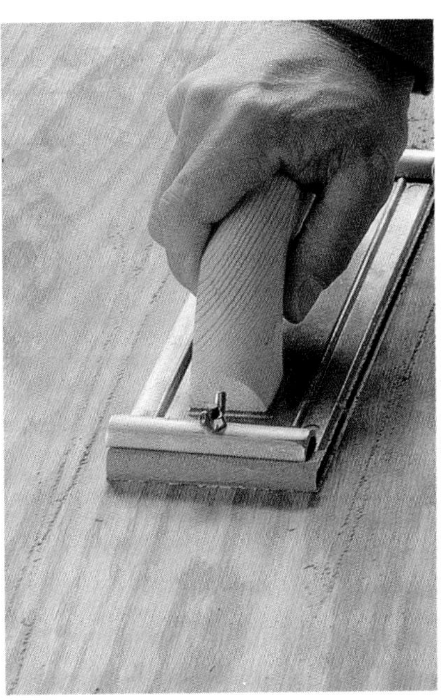

3 Lightly hand-sand the surface, following the direction of the grain, with 320-grit sandpaper. Clean thoroughly with a cloth dampened in mineral spirits before applying the finish.

A well-chosen, properly applied color layer is the most important component of an attractive wood finish.

Coloring Wood

There are several reasons to color wood. The most common reason is to enhance the appearance of wood by showing off a fine or distinctive grain pattern or creating a beautiful wood tone. But stain and penetrating oil, the two most basic coloring agents, can accomplish more practical results as well. Using a dark color conceals uneven color in your wood and can blend together two or more different wood types—a common problem encountered in refinishing.

When selecting a coloring agent for your project, you will find a vast selection of products to choose from. There are oil-based stains, water-based stains, wipe-on gel stains, penetrating oils, one-step stain-and-sealant products...the options seem endless. To sort through the many products and make the selection that is best for your project, start by finding a color you like. Then check the specific properties of the coloring agent to determine if it is the best general type for your project. Make sure it has no compatibility problems with the topcoat you plan to use, or with any old finish materials that have not been removed (see charts, next page).

Whichever coloring agent you select, read the directions very carefully before applying it to the wood. Drying time, application techniques, and cleanup methods vary widely between products—even products that are similar. Also test the product on a wood sample similar to your project. When using a stain, apply enough coats to create the exact color shade you want (stain will become darker with each new coat that is applied). Keep a careful record of how many coats you applied for your reference when you finish the actual workpiece.

This section shows:

- Coloring with Penetrating Oil (page 61)
- Coloring with Stain (pages 62 to 63)

Penetrating Oil

Penetrating oil (often called "Danish oil" or "rubbing oil") delivers color deep into the wood for a rich-looking finish that can be buffed to form a protective surface.

Advantages:
- easy to apply
- creates very even coloration
- does not "paint over" wood grain
- compatible with most topcoats
- penetrates deeper than stain for very rich color
- can be used without a topcoat

Drawbacks:
- may fade in direct sunlight
- limited range of colors
- cannot darken color with multiple coats
- toxic fumes; flammable

Compatibility:
- avoid using with oil-based polyurethane

Recommended Uses:
- wood with attractive grain pattern
- antiques and fine furniture
- decorative items

Common Brand Names:
- Watco® Danish Oil Finish, Deft® Danish Oil Finish

Water-based Liquid Stain

Water-based liquid stain is wiped or brushed onto the wood surface to create a color layer that can be darkened with additional applications.

Advantages:
- easy to clean up, safe to use
- wide range of colors available
- can be built up in layers to control final color
- dries quickly

Drawbacks:
- can raise wood grain (requires sanding for an even surface)
- can chip or scuff if not properly topcoated

Compatibility:
- bonds well with most topcoats

Recommended Uses:
- floors
- woodwork
- previously finished furniture—can be "painted" on to cover color variations
- tabletops, eating surfaces, children's furniture and toys

Common Brand Names:
- Carver Tripp® Safe & Simple Wood Stain, Behr® Water-based Stain, Varathane Elite Wood Stain®

Oil-based Liquid Stain

Oil-based liquid traditionally has been the most common type of wood stain, but its availability and popularity are declining due to environmental factors.

Advantages:
- does not raise wood grain
- slow drying time increases workability
- permanent and colorfast
- can be built up to control color
- conditions and seals wood
- less likely to bleed than water-based stain

Drawbacks:
- harmful vapors; flammable; hard to clean
- regulated or restricted in some states
- decreasing availability
- unpleasant odor

Compatibility:
- can be used with most topcoats

Recommended Uses:
- previously stained wood
- wood finish touch-up

Common Brand Names:
- Minwax® Wood Finish, Carver Tripp® Wood Stain, Zar® Wood Stain

Gel Stain

Gel stains, usually oil-based, provide even surface color that is highly controllable due to the thickness of the product. Gel finishes are growing in popularity.

Advantages:
- very neat and easy to apply—will not run
- does not raise wood grain
- dries evenly
- can be built up to deepen color
- can be buffed to create a hard surface

Drawbacks:
- limited color selection
- more expensive than other stain types
- hard to clean up
- requires buffing between coats

Compatibility:
- can be used with most topcoats

Recommended Uses:
- woodwork and furniture with vertical surfaces
- furniture with spindles and other rounded parts

Common Brand Names:
- Bartley® Gel Stain, Behlen® Master Gel

Tips for Coloring Wood

Mask the staining area to help prevent stain from bleeding into adjacent areas. As an added precaution, lightly score along the borders of the staining area with a craft knife to cut the wood fibers so they cannot draw the coloring agent out of the staining area. Applying wood sealer (page 53) also makes it easier to keep wood coloring agents from bleeding. See pages 102 to 103 for an example of masking a staining area.

Even out color by using dark stain, like the red mahogany stain being applied to this stripped door. Some wood is discolored after stripping, and using a darker stain is an easy alternative to spending hours or even days sanding the wood to completely remove all of the stain. Because it forms a more opaque color layer, wood stain is generally a better product than penetrating oil for covering wood problems.

Test coloring agents on an inconspicuous area of the workpiece to see how the color will look once the stain is applied and dry. Coloring agents often have a very different appearance on the actual workpiece than on color chips at the store display.

Seal exposed end grain with sanding sealer, then sand lightly with 220-grit sandpaper. Unsealed end grain absorbs more stain than face grain, causing it to look darker. Be careful to keep sealer off the face-grain areas.

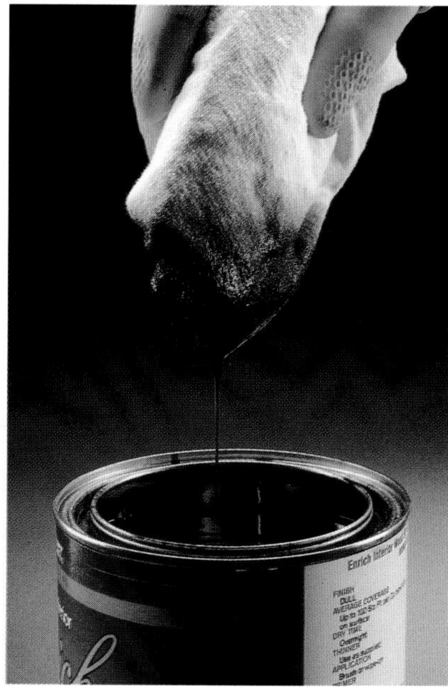

Use a clean, lint-free cloth when wiping penetrating oil or stain onto wood surfaces. Rags from well-worn cotton T-shirts make excellent staining cloths.

Coloring with Penetrating Oil

Penetrating oil is an excellent product for creating even, natural wood tones that do not obscure the wood grain. Often called Danish oil or rubbing oil, most penetrating oil is fortified with tung oil or other hardening agents that allow it to be buffed to a hard surface after application. When applied to decorative items and furniture that does not receive a significant amount of wear, penetrating oil can be used without a topcoat for a deep, low-luster finish.

When using penetrating oil, be sure to follow the manufacturer's recommendations for application and drying time. In some woods, oil finishes will seep out of wood pores for up to 72 hours while the finish dries.

Apply penetrating oil in heavy coats, using a clean staining rag.

Everything You Need:

Materials: staining cloths, tinted penetrating oil, fine abrasive pads.

How to Color Wood with Penetrating Oil

1 Prepare for the stain (page 60), then apply a heavy coat of penetrating oil to all surfaces, using a staining cloth. Wait 15 to 30 minutes, recoating any areas that begin to dry out. Apply oil to all surfaces, and let it soak into the wood for 30 to 60 minutes.

2 Wipe the surface dry with a clean cloth, rubbing with the wood grain. Apply another coat of oil with a clean cloth, then let the oil dry overnight. NOTE: Two coats are sufficient in most cases, since further coats will not darken the finish color.

3 Dab a few drops of penetrating oil onto a fine abrasive pad, then rub the surfaces until smooth. Let the oil dry for at least 72 hours before applying a topcoat. If you do not plan to topcoat the finish, buff with a soft cloth to harden the oil finish.

Creating consistent color is easy with stain, especially gel stain (above), which clings to awkward surfaces without pooling.

Coloring with Stain

"Wood stain" is a general term describing a number of different coloring agents with very different properties (page 59).

Oil-based or water-based, in liquid form or as a gel, stain is a very controllable coloring agent. The color often can be lightened by scrubbing, and it usually can be darkened by applying additional coats.

Before staining, seal all end grain and test the stain color (page 60).

Everything You Need:

Tools: paint brushes.

Materials: sanding sealer, staining cloths, liquid or gel stain, fine abrasive pads, sandpaper.

How to Apply Liquid Stain

1 Prepare for the stain (page 60), then stir the stain thoroughly and apply a heavy coat with a brush or cloth. Stir the stain often as you work. Let the stain soak in for about 15 minutes (see manufacturer's directions).

2 Remove excess stain with a clean, lint-free cloth. Wipe against the grain first, then with the grain. If the color is too dark, try scrubbing with water or mineral spirits. Let the stain dry, then buff with a fine abrasive pad.

3 Apply light coats of stain until the desired color tone is achieved, buffing with an abrasive pad between coats. Buff the final coat of stain before top-coating.

How to Apply Gel Stain

1 Prepare for the stain (page 60). Stir the gel stain, then work it into the surfaces of the workpiece with a staining cloth, using a circular motion. Cover as much of the workpiece as you can reach with the staining cloth, recoating any areas that dry out as you work. Gel stain penetrates better if it is worked into the wood with a brush or rag, rather than simply wiped onto the wood surface.

2 Use a stiff-bristled brush, like this stenciling brush, to apply gel stain into hard-to-reach areas, where it is difficult to use a staining cloth.

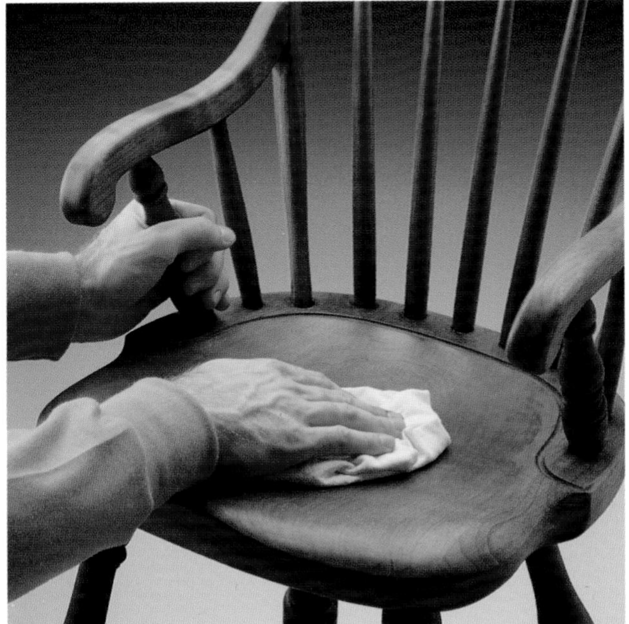

3 Let the stain soak in (see manufacturer's directions), then wipe off the excess with a clean rag, using a polishing motion. Buff the stained surface with the wood grain, using a soft, clean cloth.

4 Apply additional coats of stain until the workpiece has reached the desired color tone. Gel stain manufacturers usually recommend at least three coats to provide a thick stain layer that helps protect the wood against scratches and other surface flaws. Let the stain dry, then buff with a fine abrasive pad before applying a topcoat.

Painting Wood

Most do-it-yourselfers take on refinishing projects to preserve or showcase natural wood tones, so painting is a finishing option that is sometimes overlooked. However, it can be a helpful, timesaving solution to many refinishing problems.

Use paint as an alternative to wood stain to give plain wood a splash of color or a decorative touch; or simply use it to hide wear, low-quality materials, or unattractive wood.

Furniture and woodwork generally should be painted with water-based or oil-based enamel paint—except when using a few decorative painting techniques that call for flat wall paint (pages 68 to 69). Enamel paint forms a tough, protective coat that resists moisture, chipping, and scratching. It is available in dozens of premixed colors, and in gloss and semi-gloss versions. Or, you can have special colors custom-mixed at a paint store.

This section shows:

- Applying Paint (pages 66 to 67)
- Decorative Painting (pages 68 to 69)

Paint brushes for wood include straight trim brushes for flat areas, and tapered brushes for edges. Use synthetic brushes (nylon or polyester bristles) for both water-based and oil-based paint.

Water-based Paint

Water-based paint for wood is usually sold as "latex enamel" or "acrylic enamel." Because water-based paint can raise wood grain, use a water-based primer to prepare the wood, then sand the primed surface before applying the paint. The coloring agents in water-based paint settle quickly, so stir the paint often as you work.

Advantages:
- safer for the environment
- less toxic than oil-based paints
- easy cleanup with soap and water
- dries quickly
- can be thinned with water

Drawbacks:
- raises wood grain
- scratches easily
- cleanup is difficult after paint dries
- softens with exposure to moisture
- cannot be applied in thick coats

Compatibility:
- will not adhere to most topcoats
- may be used over other water-based paints

Recommended Uses:
- children's toys and furniture
- cabinetry
- woodwork

Oil-based Paint

Oil-based paint (also called alkyd paint) dries to a harder finish than water-based paint and offers the best protection for wood that is exposed to wear. It is still the preferred paint type of most professional painters, but this preference is changing as water-based paints become stronger and more versatile. Use oil-based primer with oil-based paint.

Advantages:
- hard, scratch-resistant finish
- unaffected by moisture
- does not raise wood grain
- dries to a very smooth finish

Drawbacks:
- releases toxic vapors
- slow drying time
- requires mineral spirits for cleanup
- use is restricted in some states

Compatibility:
- may be applied over varnish or oil-based polyurethane
- may be used over oil- or water-based paints

Recommended Uses:
- stairs and railings
- floors and doors
- woodwork
- previously finished wood

Painting Tips

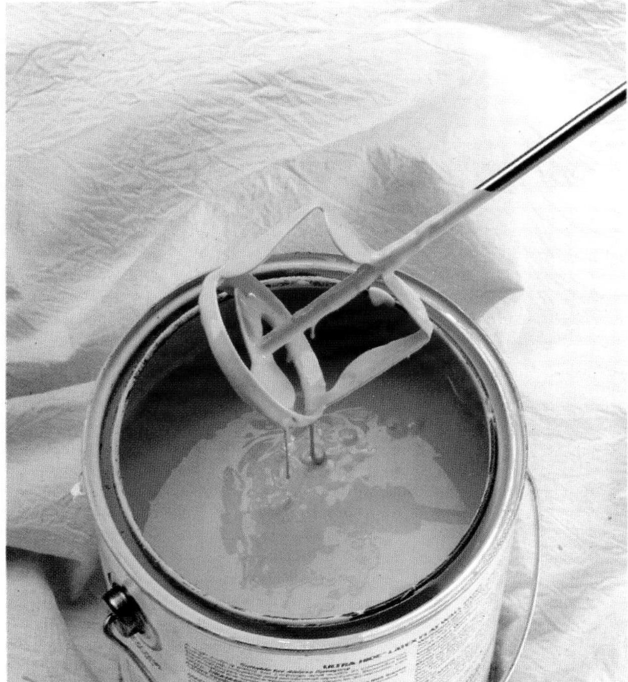

Stir paint with a mixing bit attached to a portable drill for fast, thorough mixing. Keep the mixer bit moving constantly. Repeatedly lower the mixer blade to the bottom of the can, then raise it to the top of the can to mix in settled pigment.

Strain paint to remove lumps, dirt, and other foreign materials from paint. Commercial paint strainers are available, or you can make your own from cheese-cloth or nylon stockings.

For a smooth surface free from lap marks, hold your paint brush at a 45° angle, and apply just enough pressure to flex the bristles slightly.

Applying Paint

Painting wood is very much like painting walls and other common do-it-yourself painting projects. Whenever you paint anything, preparation is critical. For wood, that means sanding the surface until it is flat and smooth, then sealing with primer so the paint absorbs evenly (see *Tips,* below). Although it is a different product, primer is applied using the same techniques as paint. In addition to sealing the wood, it keeps resins in the wood from bleeding through the paint layer.

Cleanup solvents, thinning agents, drying time, and coverage vary widely from one enamel paint to another. Read the manufacturer's directions carefully. For best results, designate a clean, dust-free area for painting (pages 30 to 33).

Everything You Need:

Tools: paint brushes, sanding block.

Materials: primer, paint, clean rags, tack cloth, sandpaper, masking tape, polyurethane.

Tips for Preparing Wood for Painting

Previously painted wood can be repainted without priming, but if the old painted surface is badly chipped or damaged, primer is helpful. Fill scratches and nicks with wood putty (pages 54 to 57), and sand the surface smooth before painting.

Clear finished wood should be stripped and sanded before priming (pages 42 to 43). Paint will not adhere well to most topcoat finishes.

How to Paint Wood

1 Finish-sand the wood (pages 56 to 57). Vacuum the surfaces or wipe with a tack cloth after you sand to remove all traces of sanding dust from the workpiece.

2 Prime the wood with an even coat of primer (use water-based primer with water-based paint, and oil-based primer with oil-based paint). Smooth out brush marks as you work, and sand with 220-grit sandpaper when dry.

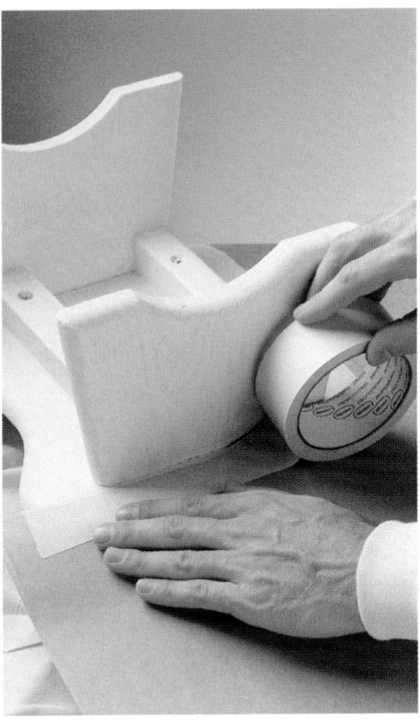

3 Mask any adjacent areas that will be painted a different color, using masking tape. Press the edges of the tape firmly against the wood.

4 Apply a thin coat of paint, brushing with the grain. When dry, sand with 400-grit sandpaper, then wipe with a tack cloth. Apply at least one more heavier coat, sanding and wiping with a tack cloth between additional coats. Do not sand the last coat.

OPTION: Apply clear polyurethane topcoat to surfaces that will get heavy wear. Before applying, wet-sand the paint with 600-grit wet/dry sandpaper, then wipe with a tack cloth. Use water-based polyurethane over latex paint, and oil-based over oil-based paint.

Decorative Painting

Apply a creative touch to your project with decorative painting techniques. Farmhouse finishes, stencil finishes, and color washes are techniques that give furniture and decorative items a rustic, Early American look. A handful of specialty paint brushes, some quality finishing materials, a few helpful tools, like stencils, and a little creativity are all you need to create these unique painted finishes on your project.

Farmhouse finishes re-create the look of worn paint. Apply a base coat of wood stain, followed by a topcoat of shellac. Paint a layer of water-based paint over the dried shellac. Once the paint is dry, sand off randomly chosen areas of paint with 100-grit sandpaper, applying varying degrees of pressure to imitate natural wear. Sand the corners of the workpiece and any detail areas with 220-grit sandpaper, then wipe with a lint-free cloth and denatured alcohol to complete the farmhouse finish.

Stenciled designs add a bright, decorative touch to topcoated or painted wood. Purchase clear acetate stencils at a craft store (or cut your own). Position the stencil on the wood, and secure it with tape. Stipple the wood by dabbing paint (acrylic craft paints are a good choice for stenciling) onto the surface through the stencil, using a stenciling brush. Allow the paint to dry before removing the stencil. If more than one color will be used, realign the stencil and apply each color, one at a time (start with the lightest color).

Color washes produce a thin, semi-transparent coat of paint on bare wood. Dilute water-based paint by mixing one part paint to four parts water (the more diluted the paint mixture, the thinner the paint layer will be). Brush the thinned paint onto the wood, working with the grain. Wipe the surface immediately with a lint-free cloth, removing paint until you achieve the desired color tone. Repeat the process to darken the color, if needed. Soften the look by scuffing the painted surface with a fine abrasive pad when dry.

Protect your finish and wood with a topcoat layer, like the wipe-on tung oil being applied to this dresser.

Applying Topcoats

Topcoat finishes seal the wood, protect the finish from scratches and other wear, and increase the visual appeal of the wood. Because they dry clear, topcoats highlight the coloring and natural figure of the wood. For most projects, a topcoat of tung oil finish, polyurethane, or paste wax will give your wood the protection it needs and the finished appearance you desire.

When choosing a topcoat, consider durability, sheen, and compatibility with any coloring layers you use (see opposite page). Other factors, like drying time, ease of application and cleanup, and safeness, should also influence your choice. If possible, check samples at building centers or paint stores to see if a particular topcoat is suitable for your workpiece.

Some one-step stain-and-seal products are also available. Test these products on scrap wood before using them on good furniture.

This section shows:

- Applying Tung Oil Finishes (page 73)
- Applying Polyurethane (pages 74 to 77)
- Applying Wax (pages 78 to 79)

Make tack cloths by moistening cheesecloth in mineral spirits. Apply a spoonful of varnish (or any other clear topcoat material) to the cheesecloth, and knead the cloth until the varnish is absorbed evenly. Make several tack cloths and store them in a glass jar with a lid.

Tung Oil Finish

Tung oil is a natural oil drawn from the nut of the tung tree. Good for creating a matte or glossy hand-rubbed finish, tung oil products are available in clear and tinted form.

Advantages:
- easy to apply
- flexible finish that resists cracking
- very natural appearance that makes minimal changes in wood appearance
- penetrates into the wood
- easily renewed and repaired

Drawbacks:
- not as durable as other topcoats

Compatibility:
- not compatible with polyurethane

Recommended Uses:
- uneven surfaces like chairs and other furniture with spindles
- woodwork
- antiques
- wood with highly figured grain

Common Brand Names:
- Minwax® Tung Oil Finish, Zar® Tung Oil, Tung Seal by McCloskey®

Water-based Polyurethane

Water-based polyurethane is an increasingly popular topcoat because of its fast drying time and easy cleanup. Its hazard-free disposal and low toxicity are a plus.

Advantages:
- fast drying time
- easy cleanup
- nonflammable
- nontoxic
- impervious to water and alcohol

Drawbacks:
- can raise wood grain
- can have an unnatural "plastic" appearance

Compatibility:
- do not apply over other topcoats, or directly over commercial sanding sealer

Recommended Uses:
- floors
- interior woodwork and furniture
- children's furniture and toys
- tabletops, eating surfaces

Common Brand Names:
- EnviroCare®, Varathane® Diamond Finish, Carver Tripp® Safe & Simple, Zar® Polyurethane

Oil-based Polyurethane

Traditionally, polyurethane has been an oil-based product. Despite the emergence of water-based polyurethanes, many refinishers still prefer this more familiar product.

Advantages:
- easier to get a smooth finish than with a water-based polyurethane
- forms durable, hard finish
- impervious to water and alcohol

Drawbacks:
- slow drying time
- disposal and use closely regulated in some states
- decreasing availability
- difficult cleanup
- toxic
- gives off smelly fumes

Compatibility:
- not compatible with other topcoats

Recommended Uses:
- furniture
- surfaces where a very thick, durable topcoat is desired

Common Brand Names:
- Defthane by Deft®, Heirloom Varnish by McCloskey®, Minwax® Polyurethane

Paste Wax

Paste wax is a blend of natural waxes, dissolved with mineral spirits or naphtha. It is favored for its hand-rubbed sheen and natural appearance.

Advantages:
- easy to renew with fresh coats
- very natural appearance
- can be buffed to desired sheen
- can be applied over most topcoats

Drawbacks:
- easily scratched and worn away
- needs to be restored regularly
- water or alcohol spills will damage wax

Compatibility:
- no restrictions

Recommended Uses:
- antiques
- fine furniture
- floors

Common Brand Names:
- Antiquax®, Johnson & Johnson® Paste Wax, Minwax® Paste Finishing Wax

Tips for Applying Topcoats

Stir topcoat finishes gently with a clean stir stick. Shaking the container or stirring too vigorously can create air bubbles that cause pockmarks in the finish when dry.

Transfer leftover topcoat materials to smaller containers to minimize the amount of air that can react with the product. Tung oil and polyurethane are especially susceptible to thickening when exposed to air.

Sand between topcoat layers, using 600-grit wet/dry sandpaper, to smooth out the finish. Wipe down the worksurface with a tack cloth after sanding. Save time and ensure better results by creating a clean, dust-free work area (pages 30 to 33). NOTE: See product label; topcoat requirements will vary.

Wet-sand with a fine abrasive pad on the final topcoat layer to create a finish with the exact amount of gloss you want.

Applying Tung Oil Finishes

Tung oil is an extremely popular finish, both for its easy application and its appearance. Several well-buffed coats applied with a clean cloth will form a suitably hard finish. With added coats and more buffing, you can achieve a glossy finish. Tung-oil-based products are suitable for most furniture, including antiques. Seldom sold in pure form, tung oil is usually blended with tinting agents or other topcoats, and is usually described by manufacturers as "tung oil finish."

Because tung oil forms a relatively thin coat, renew finished surfaces with a fresh coat of tung oil every year or so. Or, you can apply a protective layer of paste wax to guard the finish, and renew the wax topcoat periodically. Use lemon oil to refresh a tung oil finish without recoating.

Everything You Need:

Tools: assorted paint brushes.

Materials: clean cloth, rubber gloves, mineral spirits, tung oil finish, abrasive pads.

Use a paint brush to apply tung oil to very uneven surfaces. Because the excess tung oil is wiped off before it dries, there is no need to worry about lap marks from brushes.

How to Apply Tung Oil Finish

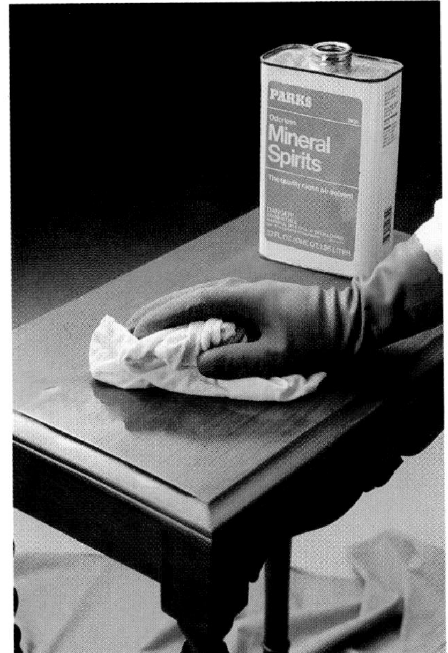

1 Clean the surfaces thoroughly with a cloth and mineral spirits. Apply a thick coat of tung oil finish with a cloth or brush. Let the tung oil penetrate for 5 to 10 minutes, then rub off the excess with a cloth, using a polishing motion.

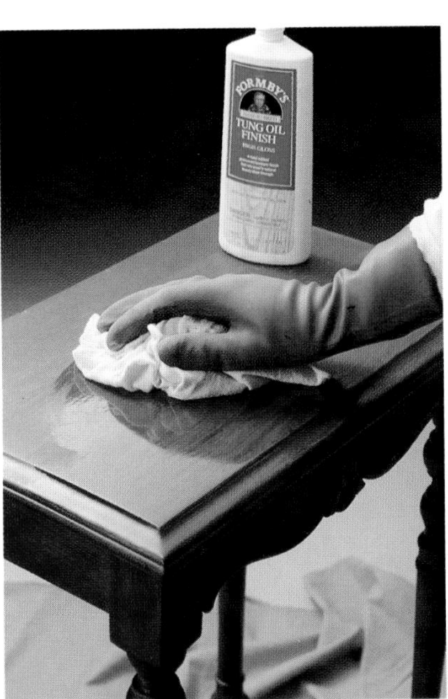

2 Buff the tung oil with a clean cloth after 24 hours, then reapply additional coats, as needed, to build the desired finish—three coats is generally considered the minimum for a good finish. Use a clean cloth for each application.

3 Let the finish dry completely, then buff it lightly with a fine abrasive pad. For a higher gloss, buff with a polishing bonnet and portable drill (page 28).

Applying Polyurethane

For safe use and low toxicity, water-based polyurethane is an excellent choice. Use it for children's furniture and toys, as well as for eating surfaces.

Polyurethane (often called polyurethane varnish or simply varnish) is a hard, durable topcoat material commonly used on floors, countertops, and other heavy-use surfaces. Available in both water-based and oil-based form (page 71), polyurethane is a complex mixture of plastic resins, solvents, and drying oils or water, that dries to a clear, nonyellowing finish.

A wide array of finishing products contain some type of polyurethane, which can cause a good deal of confusion. If a label uses the descriptive terms "acrylic" or "polymerized," the product is most likely polyurethane-based. Your safest bet in choosing the best polyurethane product for the job is to refer to the suggestions for use on the product label.

Everything You Need

Tools: vacuum cleaner, painting pad with pole extension, paint brushes.

Materials: polyurethane, mineral spirits, medium and fine abrasive pads, felt pad, staining cloths.

Tips for Choosing Polyurethane Products

Choose the finish gloss that best meets your needs. Product availability has expanded among polyurethane products in recent years to include gloss, semi-gloss, and matte (or satin) sheens. Because of the expanding product lines, polyurethane-based topcoat products have almost completely replaced traditional wood varnish.

Hardening agents are available for some brands of water-based polyurethane for outdoor applications or high-traffic areas. Hardening agents lose their effectiveness quickly, so harden only as much product as you plan to apply in one coat.

Tips for Using Polyurethane

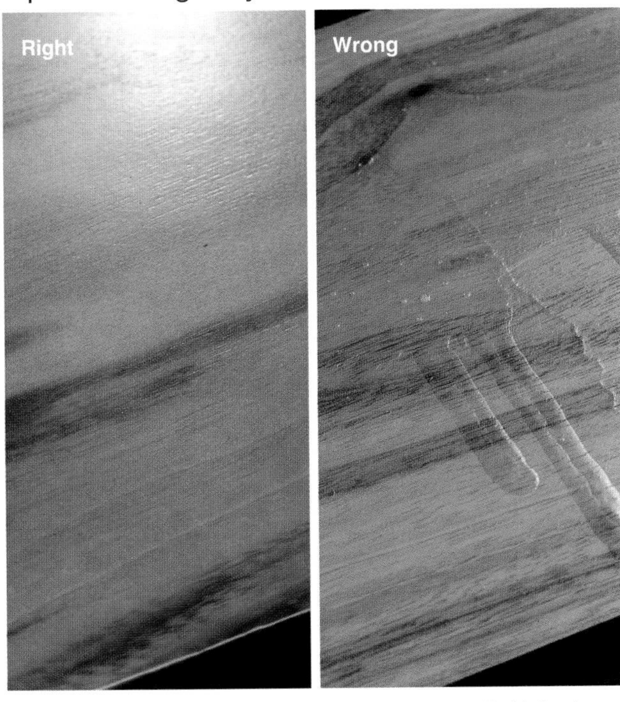

Apply polyurethane in several thin layers (left) for best results. Applying too much finish at once (right) slows down the drying time, and causes running, wrinkling, or sagging.

Brush out lap marks to create a smooth surface before the polyurethane dries. Small brush marks will show, but will blend together as the finish dries. Because it dries slowly, oil-based polyurethane gives you more time to brush out lap marks.

Examine the surface after each coat of polyurethane dries, using a bright side light. Wet-sand with a fine abrasive pad to remove dust and other surface problems, like air bubbles. After sanding, wipe the surface clean with a tack cloth.

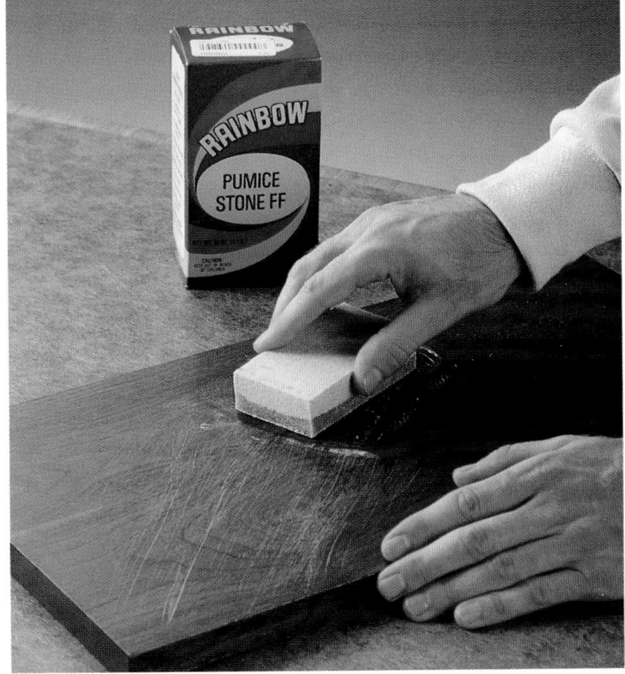

Wet-sand with fine pumice powder as a maintenance technique for removing scratches and scuffs in a hardened polyurethane finish. Sprinkle the pumice powder over the surface flaw, then rub with a felt pad or a cloth dipped in mineral spirits.

How to Apply Polyurethane to Furniture

1 Seal unstained wood with a 1:1 mixture of polyurethane and thinning agent (check product label), applied with a clean cloth or brush. Let the sealer dry. Wipe off excess sealer with a clean cloth. NOTE: Furniture that has been colored with stain or penetrating oil does not need a seal-coat.

2 Apply a coat of polyurethane, starting at the top of the project and working your way down. Use a good-quality brush. When the surface is covered, smooth out the finish by lightly brushing in one direction only, parallel to the grain. Let dry, then sand between coats, using 600-grit wet/dry sandpaper.

3 Apply the second coat. To keep the finish from running, always try to position the workpiece so the surface being topcoated is horizontal.

4 **OPTION:** After the final coat dries, wet-sand the surface with a fine abrasive pad to remove any small imperfections and diminish the gloss.

How to Apply Polyurethane to Floors

1 Seal sanded wood with a 1:1 mixture of water-based polyurethane and water, applied with a painting pad and pole extension. Let the seal coat dry, then use a medium abrasive pad to lightly buff the surfaces to remove any raised wood grain caused by the water. Vacuum the surface with a bristle attachment, or wipe with a tack cloth.

2 Apply a coat of undiluted polyurethane to the floor. Apply the finish as evenly as possible. Do not overbrush.

3 Let the finish dry, then buff the floor with a medium abrasive pad. Vacuum or wipe the floor. Apply more coats of polyurethane as needed to build the finish to the desired thickness, buffing between coats. Most floors require at least three coats of water-based polyurethane for a hard, durable finish (see manufacturer's recommendations).

4 **Option:** When the final coat of finish is dry, buff the surfaces with water and a fine abrasive pad to remove surface imperfections and diminish the gloss.

Applying Wax

Wax is an easily renewable topcoat that protects and beautifies wood. It is often applied over oil finishes and other topcoats to absorb small scratches and everyday wear and tear. Then, simply by removing the old wax and applying a fresh coat, you can create a new-looking topcoat without refinishing.

Paste wax is the best wax product for wood because it can be buffed to a hard finish. But other types of wax, like liquid wax, can be used for specific purposes.

Apply several coats of paste wax for best results. The hardness of a wax finish is a direct result of the thickness of the wax and the vigor with which it is buffed. Extensive buffing also increases the glossiness of the finish.

For the hardest possible finish, choose products with a high ratio of wax to solvent (see label).

Everything You Need:

Tools: fine abrasive pads.

Materials: paste wax, clean cloth.

Tips for Applying Wax to Furniture

Use liquid wax on detailed areas, where paste wax is difficult to apply. Apply the wax with a stiff brush, then buff with a soft cloth.

Buff wax to a hard, glossy finish with a polishing bonnet attached to a portable drill. Keep the drill moving to avoid overheating the wax.

How to Apply Paste Wax

1 Apply a moderate layer of paste wax to the wood using a fine abrasive pad or a cloth. Rub the wax into the wood with a polishing motion.

2 Allow the wax to dry until it becomes filmy in spots (above). Gently wipe off any excess, undried wax, then allow the entire wax surface to dry until filmy (usually within 10 to 20 minutes). NOTE: Do not let the wax dry too long, or it will harden and become very difficult to buff.

3 Begin buffing the wax with a soft cloth, using a light, circular motion. Buff the entire surface until the filminess disappears and the wax is clear.

4 Continue buffing the wax until the surface is hard and shiny. Apply and buff another coat, then let the wax dry for at least 24 hours before applying additional coats. Apply at least three coats for a fine wax finish.

Bright new hardware and accessories can give refinished furniture a beautiful finishing touch.

Hardware & Accessories

Restoring or replacing accessories, like hardware, glass, or upholstery, is usually the last step in the refinishing process. Give these finishing touches the same careful attention you gave to refinishing the wood.

Before you reinstall hardware or nonwood accessories, inspect their condition. Tarnished metal or worn accessories can detract from the project. Whenever possible, use the original hardware instead of replacing it, since it will match the style of the piece and fit in the original position. To find replacement parts, contact suppliers of reproduction hardware and accessories (see the manufacturer's listing on page 128). NOTE: Contact a professional before repairing or replacing electrical parts.

Sources for Replacement Items

Visit salvage yards and antique shops to search for hardware and accessories. If you can find a good match, using the authentic parts is usually preferable to using reproduction parts.

Check catalogs for reproduction parts if you are unable to find authentic hardware and accessories. Most woodworker's stores can provide information on obtaining catalogs of reproduction parts.

Order custom-made accessories for unusual and hard-to-find replacement items, like beveled glass panels. Check your phone book and local woodworker's stores for names of crafters.

Tips for Cleaning Hardware & Accessories

Use chemical strippers to remove old paint from hardware. Soak hardware in a jar of stripper, then scrub clean. Use a detail brush or an old toothbrush to get into crevices. Rinse hardware in mineral spirits, then dry immediately. Polish with metal polish and a soft cloth.

Use a wire wheel attachment on a bench grinder or portable drill to remove old paint or rust. Unlike chemical stripping, grinding off the old finish removes rust and defects, as well as old finish materials. Do not grind brass or plated metal.

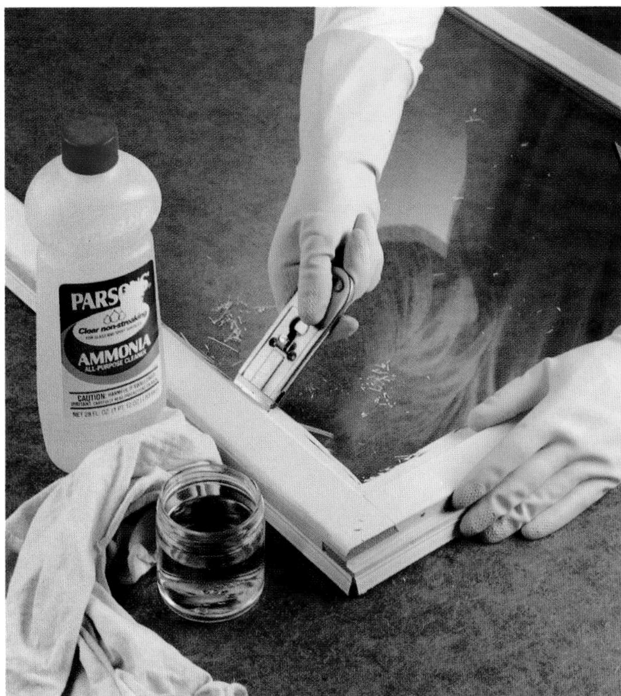

Remove paint and chemicals from glass on refinished items, using a razor blade scraper. After scraping, wash the glass with a 1:1 mixture of hot water and ammonia to remove any residue.

Test the colorfastness of upholstery before attempting to wash it. Gently rub a damp, white cloth on the fabric and look for color on the cloth. Color on the cloth indicates the fabric is not colorfast, and should be dry-cleaned. If it is colorfast, hand wash with a mild laundry detergent.

Tips for Removing & Reattaching Hardware

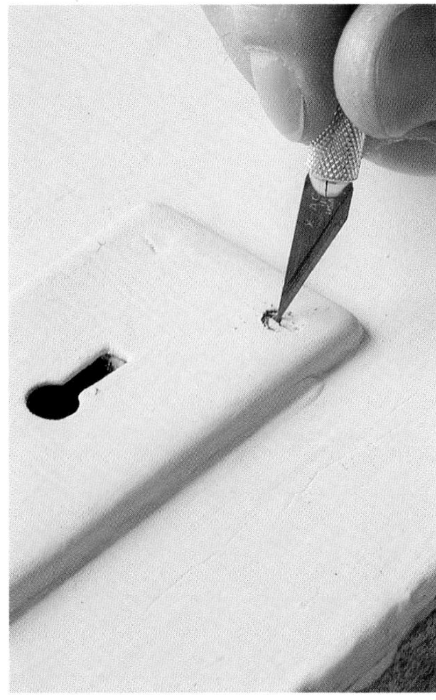

Clean paint from screw slots using a craft knife or razor blade to clear the slots for a screwdriver. Always use a screwdriver with the proper blade size to match the screw slot.

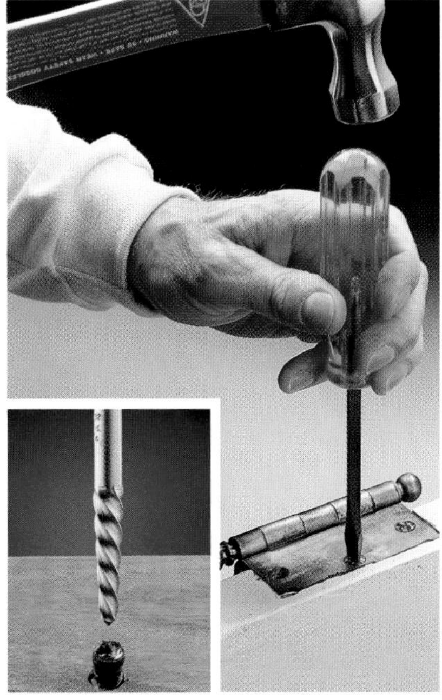

Remove stripped screws by driving a screwdriver into the slot with a sharp rap from a hammer. OPTION: To remove larger stripped screws, drill a pilot hole, then use a reverse-threaded screw extractor bit (inset photo).

Carefully slice paint between hardware plates and the wood, using a craft knife. This lets you remove hardware without extensive prying that can damage the wood and the hardware plate.

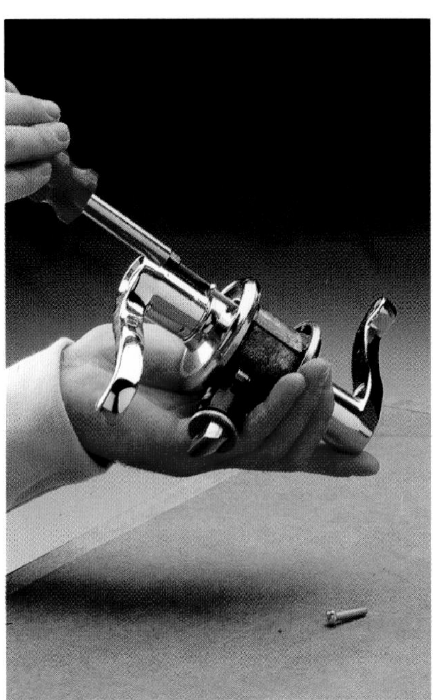

Reassemble hardware, like most doorknob-and-latch assemblies, immediately after removal so you do not lose any of the small parts.

Fill old screw holes with wood putty or filler (top). Drill new pilot holes before replacing the hardware. OPTION: Glue tapered wood plugs or dowels into screw holes to provide wood for the screw threads to grip (bottom).

Cover hardware with masking tape prior to removal to prevent damage during removal and reinstallation. One slip of the screwdriver can cause major damage to unprotected metal.

Tips for Removing & Reinstalling Glass

Protect against broken glass by taping both sides of the pane with masking tape around the edges and across the center. This will not prevent breakage, but it will hold shattered glass safely in the glass frame.

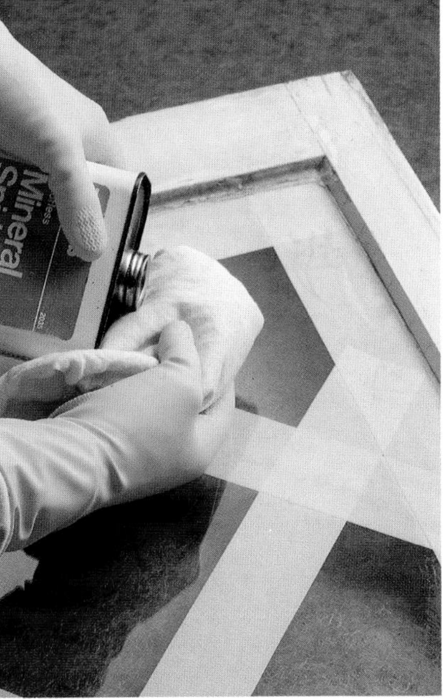

Soften hardened putty around a window frame by applying paint thinner to the putty. Scrape out the softened putty with a detail scraper (page 29) before you remove the glass panel.

Use a brad pusher, not a tack hammer, for driving brads to secure glass panels and retainer strips in furniture. Even a lightweight hammer can break glass or split retainer strips.

Tips for Reupholstering

Use seat boards or other appropriate furniture parts as a pattern for the new fabric when you are unable to use the original fabric as a pattern. Cut the new fabric slightly oversize, to allow for trimming later.

Align the fabric by marking centerpoints on the seat board. Cut a notch in the midpoint of each edge of the fabric, then align the notches with the marks on the groundwork. Secure fabric edges first, then tack down the corners.

Trim excess fabric after attaching the corners and edges.

Case Studies

Case Studies

If you show an old rocking chair to a dozen professional wood refinishers, you will probably get at least a half-dozen very different suggestions about the best way to tackle the job. Some methods may be better than others, but there is seldom only one workable solution.

Like most do-it-yourself projects, refinishing wood is essentially a series of challenges and solutions. On the following pages we have assembled a group of successful case studies in refinishing and finishing. Because there is no way to show the techniques for every imaginable project, we have presented these case studies to give you a glimpse into the decision-making process that helps determine the success or failure of each project.

To use this section, flip through the pages and note the special features of each project: the type of wood, the old finish, and any unique challenges it presents. Look for similarities between the case studies shown here and any projects you are considering. At the same time, pay close attention to the reasons behind the decisions: why did we only use a

heat gun to partially strip the surfaces? What kinds of stain were used to make two different wood types look the same?

In short, use this section to gain refinishing and finishing "experience"—but without any of the mess and fuss.

Index to Case Studies:

- Rocking Chair (pages 88 to 89)
- Sewing Machine Cabinet (pages 90 to 91)
- Kitchen Cabinets (pages 92 to 93)
- Dining Chair (pages 94 to 95)
- Chest of Drawers (pages 96 to 97)
- School Desks (pages 98 to 99)
- Frame-and-panel Cabinet (pages 100 to 101)
- Cedar Chest (pages 102 to 103)
- Antique Mantel Clock (pages 104 to 105)
- Tip-Top Table (pages 106 to 107)
- Music Cabinet (pages 108 to 109)
- Antique Radio Console (pages 110 to 111)
- Double-hung Window (pages 112 to 113)
- Woodwork & Door (pages 114 to 117)
- Wood Floor (pages 118 to 121)

Case Studies

Rocking Chair

Wood type: White oak

Old finish: Multiple layers of paint and varnish

Challenge: To strip the old, thick finish from the spindles, arms, and rungs

Solution: Apply chemical stripper, then scrub with an abrasive pad to remove topcoats; remove stain from wood using sanding cord and strips of sanding belt

Once a staple of American household furnishings, pressback rocking chairs can still be found in just about any attic or antique shop. With their trademark spindles and ornate backrest designs, these rockers present an amazing amount of detailed surface area to challenge the refinisher. But with some creative sanding and scraping tools, removing the old finish is a very manageable task. By strengthening a joint or two and applying a new finish, we were able to save our chair from an early retirement.

1 Remove the old finish (pages 36 to 43). We chemically stripped and scraped the paint and varnish in the flat areas, using a broad scraper. Then we chemically stripped the spindles, arms, legs, and rungs, using an abrasive pad to scrub off the old finish.

2 Clean up the details. We used an artists' modeling tool to scrape the finish and stripper residue from the relief design in the backrest. Because stripper softens wood, be very careful when using sharp scrapers, especially in delicate areas.

3 Make basic repairs (pages 44 to 49). The primary structural joints in our chair were sound, but a few interior spindles had loosened. We injected joint sweller into the joints at the top and bottom of each loose spindle (page 46).

4 Prepare for the finish (pages 52 to 57). We gave the chair an intermediate sanding to remove a few nicks and scratches, then filled a few larger gouges and scratches with untinted wood putty. To finish-sand the chair, we used strips from a sanding belt on the spindles and sanding cord on the grooves. It was neither necessary nor desirable to completely remove all the old color. Leaving a little bit of color in older projects creates a more natural, antique finish.

5 Color the wood (pages 58 to 63). We used a brush to apply liquid light-oak stain to the backrest and seat, but we used a rag on the spindles and the other round parts. The stain evened out the color of the chair and added richness to the wood.

6 Apply the topcoat (pages 70 to 73). Round or detailed parts are hard to finish with a paint brush, so we applied tung oil with a wiping rag. We buffed the finish with a fine abrasive pad after the third coat of oil to harden the surface.

Sewing Machine Cabinet

Wood types: Walnut and walnut veneer

Old finish: Multiple layers of paint and varnish

Challenge: To remove the old finish without damaging the veneer

Solution: Heat-strip the paint from the flat wood surface; chemically strip the veneer and the intricate parts of the cabinet

A marvel of modern engineering back in the 1940s, this electric sewing machine had become obsolete. Several poor paint jobs had transformed the cabinet into an ugly duckling that was completely forgettable. But on close examination, the hardwood cabinet was still in good condition and seemed to be worth refinishing. Now, refinished to showcase its lustrous walnut and walnut veneer, the sewing machine cabinet has reclaimed its status as a piece of fine furniture.

1 Remove the hardware (pages 80 to 82). The door pulls and the brass sewing machine hinges connecting the tabletop extension to the cabinet were covered with paint but in good operating condition. We carefully removed the hardware, including the sewing machine, for cleaning and to create better access to the wood for refinishing.

2 Remove the old finish (pages 36 to 43). We used a heat gun and scraper to strip the multiple layers of paint from the flat, solid hardwood surfaces. Once these surfaces were heat stripped we were better able to evaluate the condition of the wood, and we decided not to risk heat stripping the veneer. Stripping the larger surfaces first can give you a lot of helpful information early in the project.

3 Clean up the details. We chemically stripped the delicate carved legs and veneered doors. Specialty scrapers (page 29) made removing the sludge simple. Finally, we wiped the entire cabinet clean with an abrasive pad and denatured alcohol.

4 Prepare for the finish (pages 52 to 57). The only surface preparation required was a light sanding to help the new stain absorb evenly. We were careful to avoid oversanding the veneer on the doors, which had lovely bookmatch patterns.

5 Color and top-coat the wood (pages 58 to 63 and 70 to 79). We applied a coat of medium-tone walnut stain to enhance the wood grain and even out the color. Then we applied a three-layer topcoat of clear tung oil for a hard, antique-looking finish.

6 Clean the hardware (pages 80 to 82). We cleaned the casing of the sewing machine with a penetrating lubricant, and we soaked the hardware in chemical stripper, then scrubbed it with a brush. Buffing with brass polish put a nice gleam on all the metal.

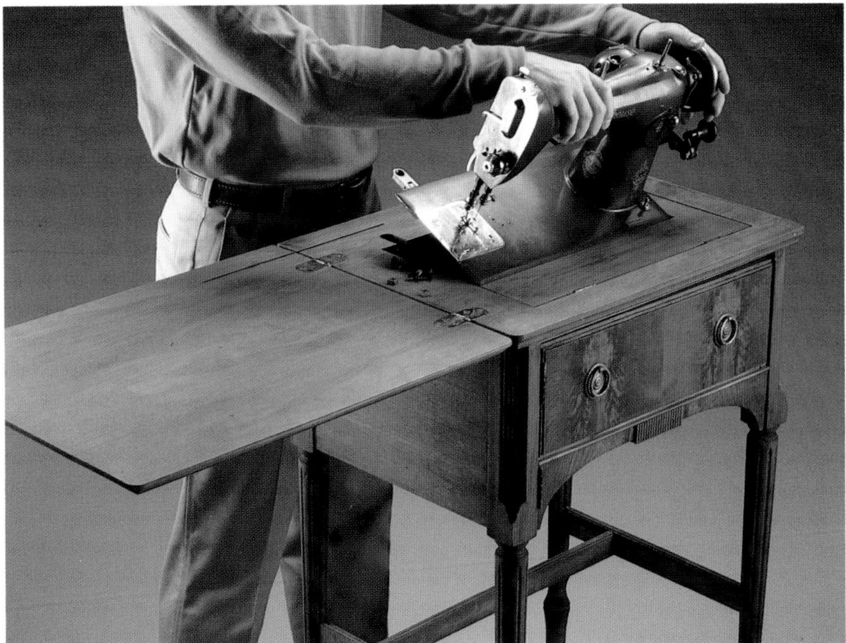

7 Reattach the hardware. To give the screws more holding power, we filled the old screw holes with wood putty and drilled new pilot holes. We considered leaving the sewing machine out to increase the storage capacity of the cabinet, but because the machine makes an interesting conversation piece, we reinstalled it in the cabinet.

Wood type:
Fir plywood

Old finish: Dark stain, varnish

Challenge: Make a plain plywood cabinet look fresh and appealing

Solution: Prepare the surfaces, and paint with light water-based paint

Case Studies

Kitchen Cabinets

These dark plywood cabinets overshadowed an otherwise light and airy kitchen. With a little preparation work and two coats of paint, we were able to spruce up the cabinets to fit into a lighter room. New brass cabinet hardware gave the cabinets the right breath of fresh air to complete the brand-new look—and without breaking the budget.

1 Remove the old finish (pages 36 to 43). We removed the hinges, latches, shelves, and doors, then scrubbed off the old varnish using mineral spirits and an abrasive pad to create a better bonding surface for the primer.

2 Prepare for the finish (pages 52 to 57). After tightening up a few loose joints (pages 44 to 49), we filled the screw holes and gouges with untinted wood putty.

3 Sand the cabinet. We used a finishing sander to smooth out roughness and unevenness in the surface. Sanding also gives "tooth" to the surface so the primer bonds better (page 66).

4 Paint with primer (pages 64 to 67). A base coat of interior latex primer sealed the wood and filled tiny nicks and scratches, creating a smooth surface.

5 Paint the cabinet, doors, and shelves. We applied two coats of semi-gloss latex paint, using a 2" nylon-bristled sash brush. We wet-sanded lightly between coats with 600-grit wet/dry sandpaper to create a smoother finish.

6 Make the finishing touches. We replaced the brass door pulls and hinges (pages 80 to 82), then hung the finished cabinet doors and installed the shelves.

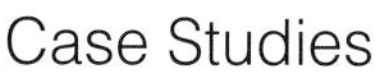

Case Studies

Dining Chair

Wood type: White oak

Old finish: Dark stain, varnish

Challenge: Fix the splintered, chipped edges of the chair legs

Solution: Use a router and roundover bit to trim away the damaged edges of the legs

Dining chairs take a real beating just from daily use. The oak dining chair shown here was no exception. When we found it, it was chipped, splintered, and dirty. Because it was no longer part of a dining-room set, we had no real restrictions on choosing a refinishing strategy for the chair. If there are matching table and chairs, you must usually refinish the entire set, because matching the other pieces can be quite difficult. If only one or two of the chairs in a set need refinishing, try using quick fixes (see pages 122 to 125) to take care of the problems.

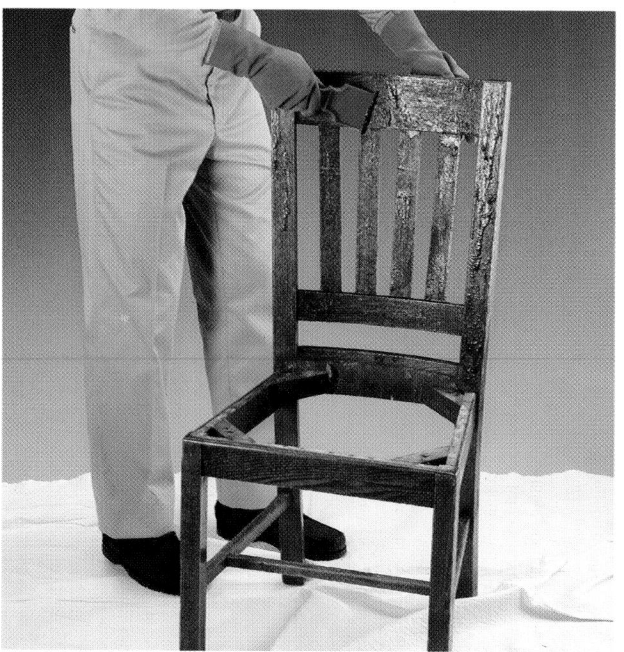

1 Remove the old finish (pages 36 to 43). After removing the seat, we used chemical stripper and scrapers to take off the old varnish (mineral spirits will dissolve pure varnish, but stripper is faster and more thorough). We wiped the chair with mineral spirits to clean off any traces of stripper or varnish.

2 Make basic repairs (pages 44 to 49). Like many older chairs, ours had become a little wobbly. We tightened the screws at the corner blocks, but the wobble persisted. So we drilled a hole through the joint that caused the wobble, then injected epoxy glue into the hole (page 46). The wobble disappeared.

3 Round over the legs. Instead of repairing the many gouges and splinters on the legs, we rounded the outside corners of the legs with a router and 3⁄8", piloted roundover bit. A plane or spokeshave also can be used, but be very careful not to remove too much wood.

4 Prepare for the finish (pages 52 to 57). We sanded the chair to get rid of a few scratches and gouges, then filled the remaining flaws with untinted wood putty. We finish-sanded the entire chair to remove some color and create a smooth surface for staining.

5 Color and top-coat the wood (pages 58 to 69 and 70 to 79). We used medium-dark walnut stain to even out the color of the wood and to give us a "Mission" type finish to match the style of the chair. To more easily top-coat the slats and crevices, we used three coats of wipe-on tung oil.

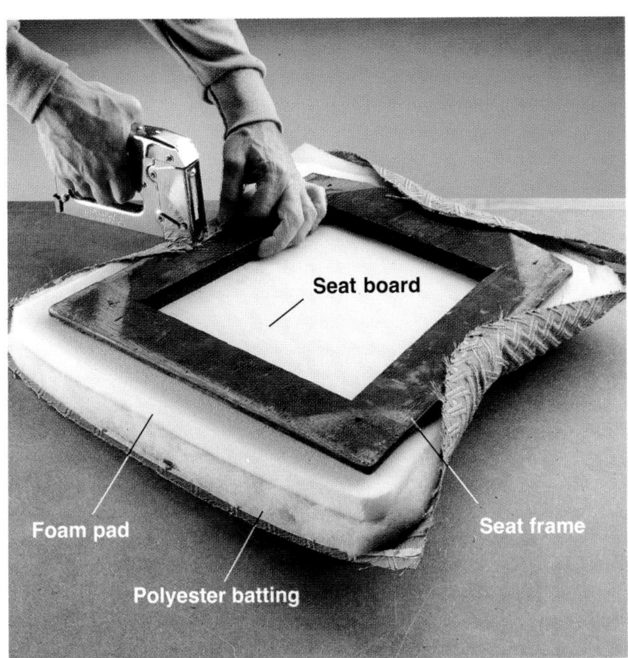

6 Reupholster the seat (page 83). We removed the old upholstery, then used the seat as a pattern to cut foam rubber and polyester batting to fit over the seat board. We chose new upholstery to complement the finish, and stapled it onto the seat frame over the batting and foam.

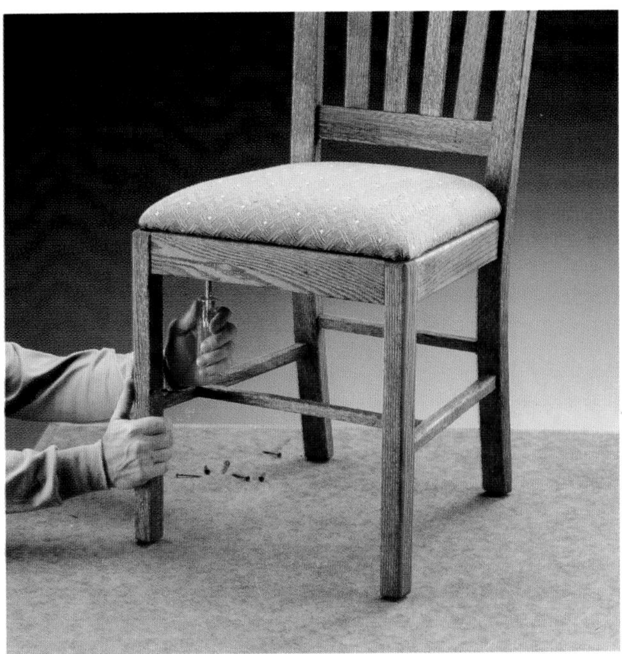

7 Reattach the seat. To secure the reupholstered seat, we drove 1½" screws through the corner braces of the chair frame and into the seat board.

Case Studies

Chest of Drawers

Wood type: Pine

Old finish: Shellac

Challenge: Tighten drawer joints

Solution: Disassemble and reglue loose joints

Pine is a very traditional wood for household furnishings, largely for its availability and rustic appearance. It is a soft, workable wood, which adds to its popularity, but makes it susceptible to damage. This chest of drawers shows what can happen to poorly protected pine. But because pine is simple to repair, we were able to restore our chest of drawers easily.

1 Remove the old finish (pages to 36 to 43). We pulled out the drawers and removed the drawer hardware first (page 82), then we scrubbed the chest carcass and the drawer fronts with a medium abrasive pad dipped in denatured alcohol—the mildest solvent that is effective on shellac.

2 Make basic repairs (pages 44 to 51). For long-lasting repairs, we disassembled the loose dovetail joints in two of the drawers, then cleaned out the old glue with a file. We glued and reassembled the joints, then clamped the drawers with pipe clamps.

3 Prepare for the finish (pages 52 to 57). We sanded the carcass and the drawer fronts with a finishing sander to eliminate many of the nicks and scratches. Then we filled the larger scratches and gouges with wood putty, and finish-sanded the carcass and the drawer fronts.

4 Color the wood (pages 58 to 63). We applied sanding sealer to the entire chest of drawers to seal the soft, absorbent wood. Then we stained the wood with a light cherry liquid stain to add interest to the pine and even out the color. We applied the stain in thin coats until we had an even finish color.

5 Apply a topcoat (pages 70 to 79). We applied semi-gloss polyurethane to the chest of drawers for a durable topcoat. We brushed on three coats, sanding with a fine abrasive pad between coats.

6 Install new hardware (pages 80 to 82). We purchased new Colonial-style drawer pulls that are very similar to the original hardware, although slightly larger. Often, metal hardware affects the color of the wood below, so it is usually best to purchase replacement hardware that is slightly larger than the original hardware. We also coated the drawer glides with beeswax for smoother operation.

Case Studies

School Desks

Wood type: Maple

Old finish: Polyurethane varnish

Challenge: Working with metal and wood parts in the same project

Solution: Disassemble for repair where needed; mask metal and wood parts while finishing

Before World War II, countless rows of these tiny desks lined the aisles of America's schoolrooms. Because the desks contain both wood and metal structural parts, completely disassembling them would have simplified our job, allowing us to work on the parts separately. But the joints were still very strong, and we did not want to weaken the desks. So we disassembled only those parts that needed repairs.

1 Disassemble the desks. We unscrewed the desk feet from the wooden runners and removed one of the maple seats because it had a crack that needed repair. We set the metal fasteners aside in a marked container for safe storage.

2 Remove the old finish (pages 36 to 43). Originally, these desks probably were top-coated with many layers of paste wax. But not long ago, a refinisher removed the wax and smothered the wood surfaces with several thick coats of polyurethane. We used a methylene chloride-based chemical stripper to cut through the polyurethane.

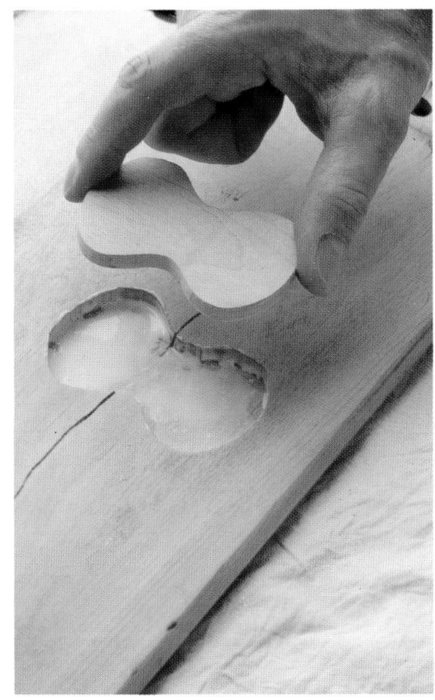

3 Make basic repairs (pages 44 to 51). We glued the crack in the seat we had removed, and reinforced the repair with a wooden mending plate (page 48). After the glue dried, we sanded out a few scratches and filled the larger ones with untinted wood putty.

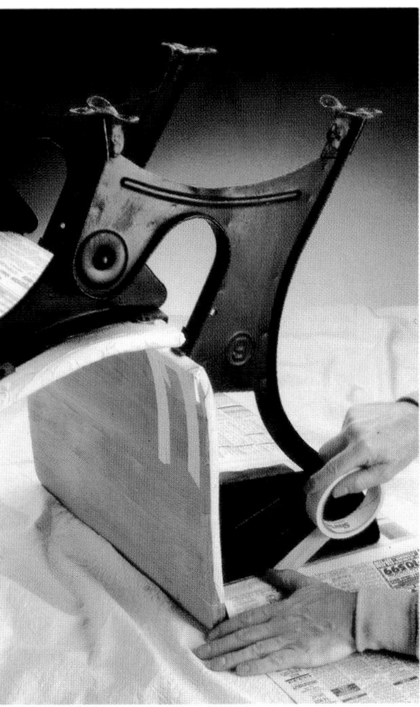

4 Mask the wood. To protect the wood from paint overspray, we masked it with tape and newspaper before we started working on the metal parts that were still attached.

5 Refurbish the metal parts. We used emery cloth to smooth out ridges and rough spots. Then we wiped the metal clean and sprayed it with primer. After the primer dried, we painted the metal with rust-inhibiting enamel spray paint.

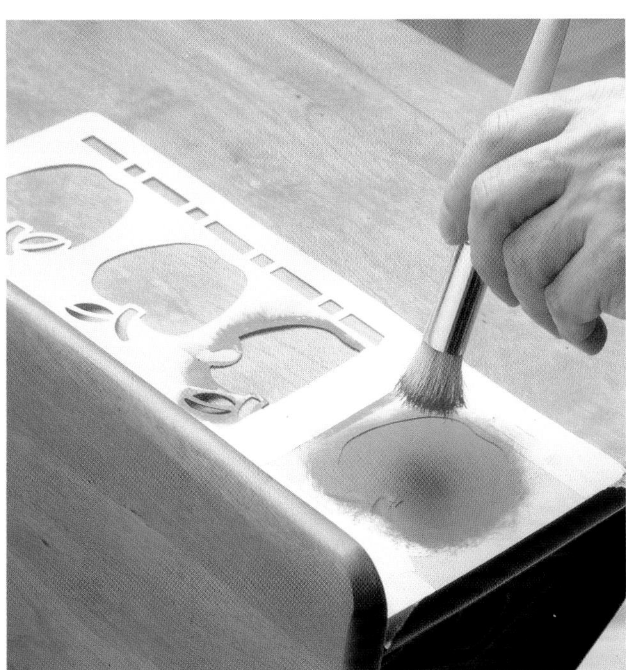

6 Finish the wood. We brushed on a thin coat of water-based polyurethane to seal the wood, then we painted stencils onto the desktops with acrylic craft paint (pages 68 to 69). After the stencils dried, we added a two-layer topcoat of water-based polyurethane (pages 76 to 77).

7 Reassemble the desks. Our school desks were mounted on wooden runners so they could be moved easily without risk of tipping over. We refinished the runners and reattached the repaired seat. Then we cleaned up the original screws and reattached the desks to the runners.

Frame-and-panel Cabinet

Wood type: Solid oak cabinet with oak veneer top

Old finish: Shellac

Challenge: Remove the old topcoat without further damaging the veneer on the cabinet top

Solution: Strip the veneer top with alcohol and the rest of the cabinet with chemical stripper

This frame-and-panel cabinet once housed an electrical appliance (probably a sewing machine) that has long since vanished. But the cabinet itself remained in good condition—a fine example of 1920s Arts-and-Crafts styling. With a few repairs and a new, lighter finish, it was ready for a second life as a unique storage cabinet.

1 Make repairs to the cabinet. An appliqué on one door was missing a section. Making a new section was a job for a woodcarver, so we removed the doors, then chiseled off the missing section's counterpart on the other door, creating a symmetrical look. We did this repair before stripping, so the wood beneath the removed appliqué section would blend in better.

2 Remove the old finish (pages 36 to 43). We used denatured alcohol and an abrasive pad to strip the old shellac from the cabinet top, which had some loose veneer on one edge. Alcohol evaporates quickly, so it is less likely than most other solvents to seep under the loose veneer and dissolve the glue.

3 Strip the doors and the body of the cabinet. We switched to a semi-paste chemical stripper for the doors and the rest of the cabinet. Semi-paste stripper clings to uneven surfaces, like the appliqués and the egg-and-dart beading on the side and back panels, without drying out or running off. We used a variety of brushes and specialty scrapers (page 29) to clean the stripper sludge from the intricate areas.

4 Repair the veneer (pages 50 to 51). Although the veneer on our cabinet top had loosened in spots, there was no significant damage. To repair it, we cleaned out beneath the veneer in the loosened areas along the edges, then injected glue under the sections. We rolled the veneer with a wallpaper roller, then covered the repair with wax paper and clamped it down to dry.

5 Apply a topcoat (pages 70 to 79). Stripping and light sanding brought out a light, even color tone to the cabinet, so we decided not to stain the wood. We simply rubbed on three layers of wipe-on gel varnish (applied like gel stain, page 63) for a clear, antique-looking topcoat.

6 Hang the doors. The frame-and-panel cabinet presented many storage possibilities: a small entertainment center, a magazine rack, or a garage for small appliances, for example. It would take only a few shelves or drawers to accommodate any of these uses. We left the cabinet open so the new owner could customize the storage area for his or her needs.

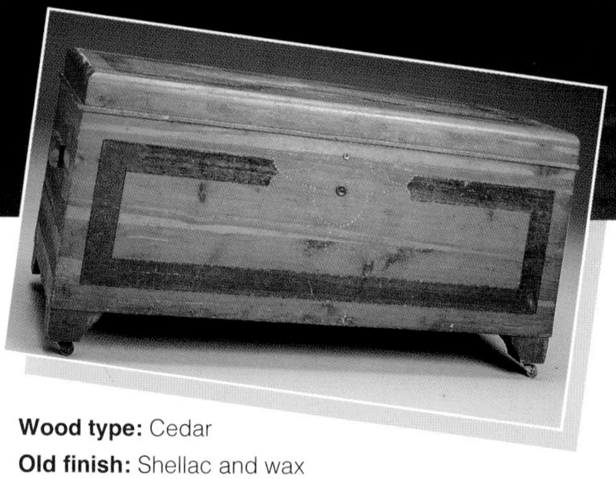

Case Studies

Cedar Chest

Wood type: Cedar

Old finish: Shellac and wax

Challenge: Renew the worn, scratched-up appearance

Solution: Sand down to bare wood and apply a new topcoat

This cedar chest is a good example of the type of project that causes a dilemma for refinishers: how to recondition a rough, worn project without sacrificing its antique charm. The chest was so worn out that fairly radical measures would be required to get it back in shape. After we removed the old topcoat, the many scratches and gouges in the chest top made it clear that the old finish had to go. So we sanded it down, and once the project was complete, we knew we had made the right decision—the gleaming new finish helped the natural beauty of the cedar chest shine through.

1 Remove the old finish (pages 36 to 43). The old, gummy shellac-and-wax finish stripped off easily with denatured alcohol and an abrasive pad, revealing the true condition of the wood.

2 Sand down to bare wood. We used a belt sander with 120-grit sandpaper on the chest top to remove most of the scratches and gouges. We used a finishing sander on the sides, front, and back.

3 Prepare for the finish (pages 52 to 57). We used wood putty to fill a large crack in the top of the chest, as well as a few small scratches and nicks that survived the first round of sanding. We tinted the stainable wood putty to match the color of the surrounding wood.

4 Apply decorative coloring (pages 58 to 63). Traditionally, cedar chests are left unstained, so we used stain only to restore the decorative banding on the top and front of the chest. To keep the stain from bleeding outside the banding areas, we cut around the outlines with a craft knife, sealed the chest with sanding sealer, and masked the adjacent areas with tape. We used red mahogany stain to re-create the banding.

5 Apply the topcoat (pages 70 to 79). We used three coats of paste wax for a hand-rubbed, antique finish. We used paste wax because it can be renewed easily if the chest becomes scratched or nicked.

6 Attach the hardware (pages 80 to 82). The roller mechanisms on our chest were too badly rusted to salvage, so we purchased new rollers from a furniture supply store. Inside the chest, we installed new chest lid supports. The hinges and the lock simply needed a little brass polish.

Case Studies

Antique Mantel Clock

Wood type: Pine cabinet with mahogany veneer

Old finish: Orange shellac

Challenge: Clean up and restore the dry, delicate wood and veneer

Solution: Strip off the old, gummy shellac with denatured alcohol and an abrasive pad

Wooden mantel clocks, like the antique "Ogee" clock shown here (Ansonia Brass & Copper Co., circa 1860), were the first mass-produced, affordable clocks. It is always a good idea to get the opinion of an antiques appraiser before you undertake any refinishing project on older items. Often, even a first-rate refinishing job will devalue a genuine antique. Because our clock no longer had the original clockwork, the "antique value" was less of a factor for us than the desire to restore the original beauty of the clock.

1 Remove the clockwork. To protect the clock mechanism, we unhooked the pendulum, then removed the hands and clock face, as well as the clockwork, which was mounted to the back panel. We also removed the door.

2 Remove the old finish (pages 36 to 43). The wood was old and brittle, so we used the gentlest solvent—alcohol—that would dissolve the old shellac. We carefully wiped up the dissolved finish with an abrasive pad.

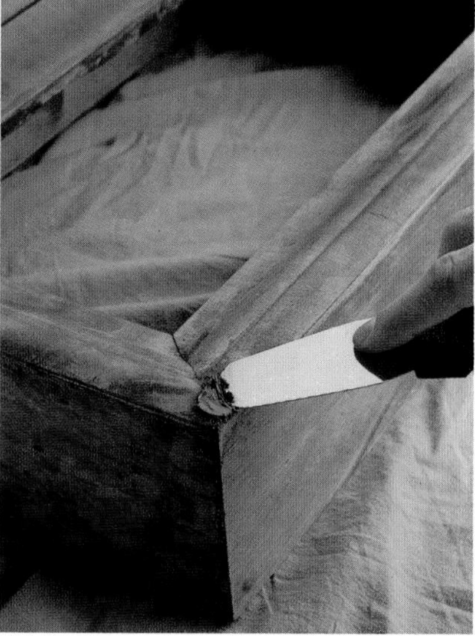

3 Prepare for the finish (pages 52 to 57). No significant repairs to the clock cabinet were needed, but we did fill in a small spot of missing veneer with stainable wood putty. We lightly hand-sanded all the wood surfaces.

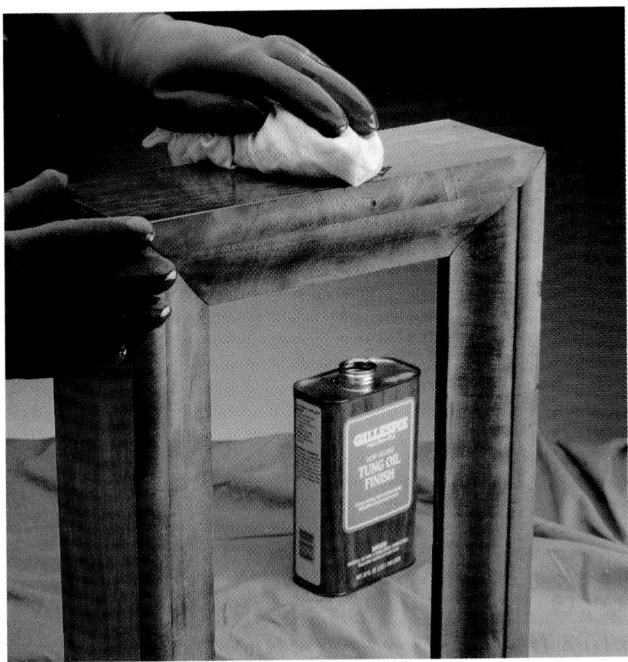

4 Apply a new topcoat (pages 70 to 79). The mahogany veneer on our clock was highly figured and relatively dark to start with, so we did not color the wood. We applied several coats of clear tung oil to all the wood surfaces. With genuine antiques, avoid using glossy topcoat finishes that can make wood look newer. The main function of the topcoat is to seal the wood and form a protective layer.

5 Strip the glass panel (pages 80 to 83). The original floral image on the lower glass panel of the door had been ravaged beyond restoration by decades of contact with the pendulum. Using water and a fine abrasive pad, we were able to wipe away the image easily, without removing the glass from the door (a risky operation with old wood).

6 Replace the artwork on the glass. To keep the clock looking as authentic as possible, we applied a golden wheat, rub-on decal to replace the floral pattern (images of Americana were very common on mantel clocks of this era). Masking the adjoining wood and back-painting the glass with black spray paint highlights and protects the new design.

7 Reassemble the clock. After cleaning and reattaching the clockwork, we tacked the back panel to the clock cabinet. We cleaned up the hinges and hung the door, replacing the old, rusty brads with #4 × ½" brass wood screws. We also resecured the paper clock face to its mounting plate, using a thin coat of rubber cement.

Case Studies

Tip-Top Table

Wood type: Mahogany

Old finish: None

Challenge: To create a superior wood finish

Solution: A 14-coat, fine finish composed of grain filler, stain, varnish, and paste wax

This *Tip-Top Table* is a reproduction of a traditional design common in the Southern United States. Manufactured as a kit by the Bartley Collection, Ltd., it features a tabletop that tilts to a near-vertical position for easy storage. Because it is made from solid mahogany, the table deserves a fine, polished finish like the 14-coat finish we applied. Although most furniture sold unfinished is sanded at the factory, a final finish sanding at home is very important.

1 Sand the tabletop (pages 56 to 57). We used a sequence of progressively finer sandpaper (150-, 180-, 220-grit) to create a smooth surface on the raw wood of our table.

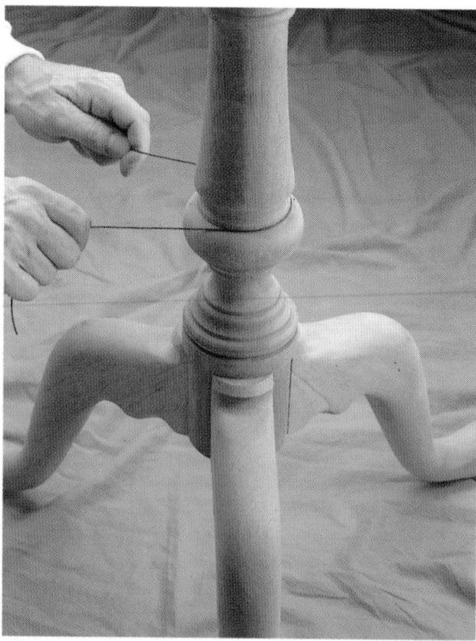

2 Sand the pedestal. We sanded the grooves in the pedestal with 150-grit sanding cord, then we hand-sanded the rest of the pedestal with 150- then 220-grit sandpaper. We wiped the table with a tack cloth after sanding.

3 Fill the grain (pages 54 to 55). We applied grain filler to the tabletop and sanding sealer to the pedestal, sanding off excess filler with 320-grit sandpaper after the filler dried. We smoothed out the sealer with 220-grit sandpaper.

4 Color the wood (pages 58 to 63). We applied brown mahogany gel stain to the entire table, including the underside of the tabletop. Applying the same finish, even in unseen areas of a project, helps prevent warping. We used gel stain because it clings well to vertical surfaces and creates very even coloration.

5 Buff the stain. A light buffing with a soft, lint-free cloth removes dust and ensures a better bond with the next coat of finish. We applied three coats of stain for the deep color we wanted over most of the table. Because the grain filler kept the stain from penetrating into the tabletop as deeply as in the pedestal, we made the color uniform by adding another coat of stain to the tabletop only.

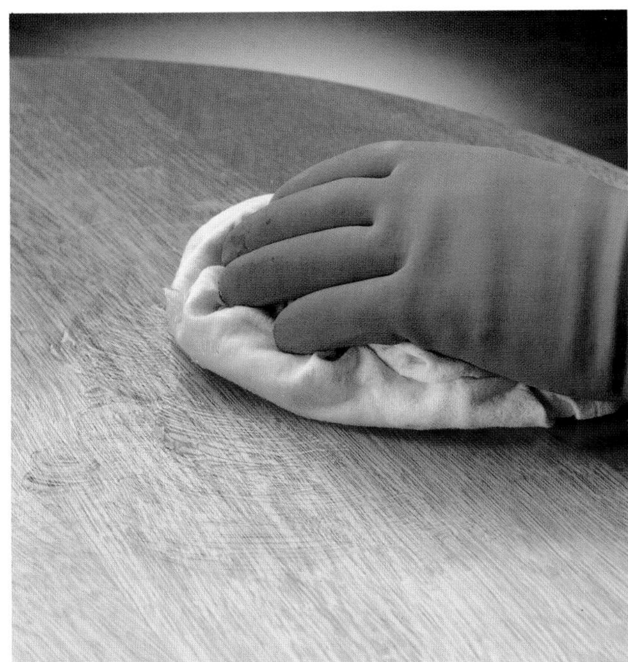

6 Apply the topcoat (pages 70 to 79). For our topcoat, we used clear gel varnish similar to the gel stain used for coloring. We applied two coats of varnish to the entire table, using the same application techniques as with the stain. To produce a deep, durable finish, we added three more coats of varnish to the tabletop.

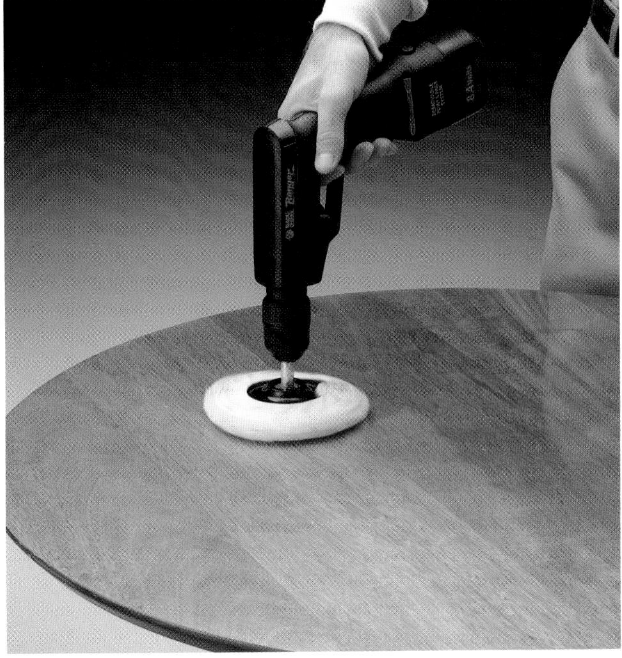

7 Apply wax and buff. We applied one well-buffed coat of paste wax on the pedestal, and four coats on the tabletop. The result was a fine, polished finish that is 14 coats thick on the tabletop, and quite beautiful to behold.

Case Studies

Music Cabinet

Wood type: Maple, others

Old finish: Shellac, others

Challenge: Even out mismatched color caused by differing wood and finish types

Solution: Chemically strip the old topcoat, sand, and apply darker stain

This unique cabinet, built to hold sheet music, is a survivor from an era when entertainment usually meant gathering around the piano for an intimate musical evening. When we found the cabinet, it had become a mismatched combination of original and replacement parts. The only thing all the wood pieces had in common was the need to be refinished. Refinishing brought a dramatic transformation, and now this off-key hodgepodge of parts is in perfect harmony.

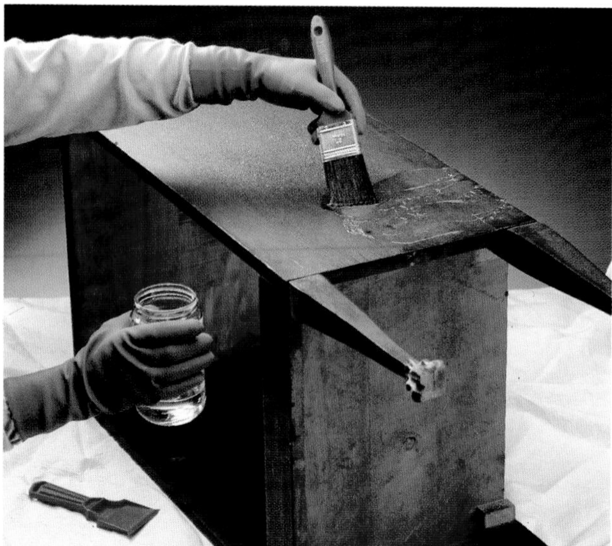

1 Remove the old finish (pages 36 to 43). Removing the door and back panel first gave us access to take out the shelves. We brushed on chemical stripper, then scraped and scrubbed off the various topcoat finishes from the cabinet and the shelves.

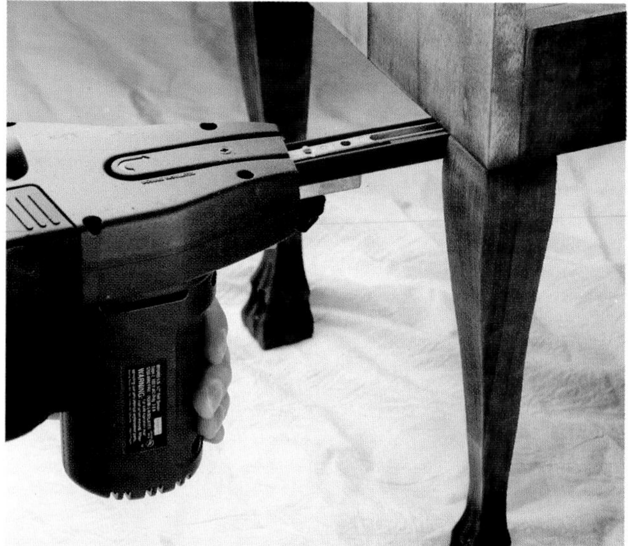

2 Prepare for the finish (pages 52 to 57). A 1/2"-belt sander worked nicely for an intermediate sanding of contoured and hard-to-reach spots. We used a finishing sander on the flat surfaces. NOTE: When using a power sander, keep the sandpaper moving constantly to avoid gouging.

3 Fill cracks in wood surfaces. We filled a few deep cracks and fractured gluelines in the sides and top of the cabinet, using untinted wood putty. Then we sanded the putty down to the surface, and stained it to match the color of the surrounding wood. We finish-sanded the entire cabinet to prepare it for the finish.

4 Apply the new finish (pages 58 to 63 and 70 to 79). Once the old finish was removed, it was even more obvious that the cabinet was composed of several different wood species. So we applied red mahogany stain, darkening the wood just enough to obscure most of the evidence of mismatched wood. Once the color was even, we applied three coats of clear tung oil for low-luster protection.

5 Finish the shelves. The cabinet shelves were in decent shape, but the wood was very dry, brittle, and drab. We stained the shelves with ebony-colored stain to contrast the cabinet, then added a tung oil topcoat, which also refreshened the dry wood.

6 Make the finishing touches. We cleaned and attached the hardware (pages 80 to 82), inserted the shelves, hung the doors, and attached the back panel. Then we applied two coats of paste wax (pages 78 to 79) and buffed the surface to give the cabinet a gentle sheen that can be renewed on a regular basis.

Case Studies

Antique Radio Console

Wood type: Poplar with walnut veneer, basswood accent trim

Old finish: Dark stain, clear shellac

Challenge: Revamp the deteriorated finish while preserving the authentic look

Solution: Strip off the topcoat, touch up the color, replace the worn grille cloth and decals with reproductions

There is nothing like an antique radio to conjure up vivid images of family and bygone days. At one time, this 1937 RCA brought a whole new brand of entertainment to an appreciative family. But when television overshadowed the radio as the main form of family entertainment, a period of neglect began for the radio, leaving it looking old and battered. A local antique radio expert provided a replica grille cloth and new decals, as well as some interesting trivia and good advice about the radio. He also updated the radio set with safer, more efficient parts.

1 Remove the radio set. Although our old radio still worked, the sound quality was poor and the brittle wiring was a fire hazard. So we unplugged the radio, took off the knobs and the back panel, disconnected the radio, and brought it to a professional for servicing.

2 Mask the fragile parts. The plastic selector cover and the trademark "eye" did not need replacing, so we masked them with masking tape to protect them from the refinishing chemicals.

3 Remove the old topcoat (pages 36 to 43). We used a medium abrasive pad and denatured alcohol to dissolve and remove the old shellac without affecting the color of the wood.

4 Color the wood (pages 58 to 63). We started by masking around the basswood accent trim, then colored the trim pieces with red mahogany stain to replicate their original color. We colored the rest of cabinet with cherry-tinted penetrating oil.

5 Apply a new topcoat (pages 70 to 79). Two coats of polyurethane gave us a hard finish that protects the veneer. We used water-based, satin-luster polyurethane to produce a less glossy, antique look.

6 Replace the grille covering. We stapled a piece of reproduction grille cloth to the backing board, then reinstalled it in the console.

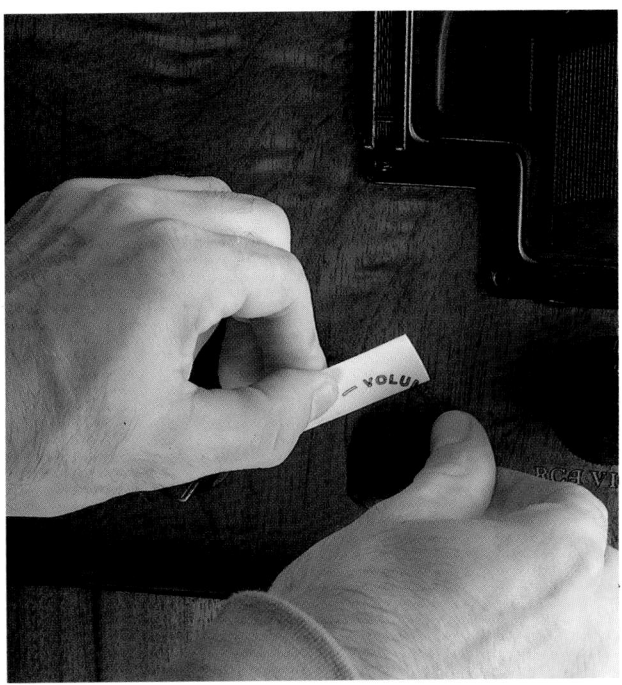

7 Apply the finishing touches. After reinstalling the radio set, we attached the knobs and applied the new decals around the radio controls (transfer-type decals should be applied after the last finish coat). We also revived the selector guard and eye with plastic cleaner.

Case Studies

Double-hung Window

Wood type: Pine

Old finish: Multiple layers of paint

Challenge: To paint the window sashes and casing without damaging the glass or impeding the smooth operation of the window

Solution: Remove the sashes and strip off the old paint to avoid paint buildup

Window sashes and casings need refinishing more frequently than just about any other part of a house. Exposure to moisture and sunlight and the friction of sliding sashes take their toll in a hurry. Many homeowners simply cover the window with coat after coat of fresh paint. The result is windows that stick—especially in warmer, more humid weather. To keep this from happening to our window, we disassembled it and stripped the old paint from the casing and the sashes. It took some time and effort, but now our window looks great and operates smoothly.

1 Protect the glass. Taping over each panel with masking tape protects the glass from finish materials and increases its shock resistance against breakage (page 83).

2 Disassemble the window. Stripping and finishing the window sashes in place is convenient, but some sash parts cannot be reached while the window is still intact. We removed the stop molding that keeps the sashes on track, then we disconnected the spiral sash springs and removed both window sashes. We also removed the sash lock and the pull.

3 Remove the old finish (pages 36 to 43). We heat-stripped the casing and the stop molding, and chemically stripped the sashes (do not use heat guns near glass or plastic). Because we planned to paint the window, we were not too concerned with removing every last bit of old paint. More importantly, we wanted to remove enough paint to prevent any problems caused by paint buildup.

4 Prepare for the finish (pages 52 to 57) and paint the sashes (pages 64 to 69). We sanded the wood to feather out any unevenness and create a better bond. A coat of sanding sealer helped ensure even absorbency for the paint. Using a tapered sash brush, we painted the interior sides of the sashes with interior latex paint to complement the color scheme in the room, and we painted the exterior sides with exterior latex to match the house trim.

5 Paint the casing. We used a 2" brush with polyester bristles to paint the casing and the stop molding. A paint shield positioned next to the jambs kept the paint off the adjoining wall. We applied two coats of paint to all parts of the window. TIP: Wipe both sides of the paint shield regularly with a water-dampened rag when using latex paint (dampen the rag with mineral spirits when using oil-based paint).

6 Hang the sashes. We reattached the sash lock and the pull, then set the painted sashes back into the window and attached the stop molding, painting over the sash-molding screws so they would blend in. Finally, we reconnected the sash springs in the tracks.

Woodwork & Door

Wood type: Red oak woodwork and fir door

Old finish: Varnish and paint

Challenge: Create matching finishes from two different wood types

Solution: Strip and scrape the old finish; use different stain colors on the door and the woodwork to create matching finish colors

Furniture can be removed and wood floors can be covered, but the interior woodwork in your house cannot be hidden. The owner of the house shown here wanted to restore his woodwork and doors to their natural wood color. But like many homeowners, he feared that stripping the paint and refinishing the woodwork would be too difficult and very time-consuming. However, by using the best techniques and materials, even refinishing woodwork and doors can be done with relative ease and economy.

It is not uncommon for a home to contain woodwork and doors made of different wood types, as is the case with our featured home. The finish-removal method we selected was the same for both the woodwork and the doors—heat-strip to remove most of the old paint, then chemically strip and scrape off the rest. But the real challenge lay in the finishing. After some experimenting, we found a combination of stain colors that, when applied to the different wood types, produced a uniform color on all the wood.

1 Remove the door and mask off the work area. We attached plastic to all the door jambs in our work area to keep fumes and dust out of the rest of the house. The hinges and other door hardware were removed, as were the switchplates and receptacle covers close to the work area. SAFETY TIP: Mask the switches and receptacles immediately after the plates are removed to avoid the risk of electric shock.

2 Remove the old finish (pages 36 to 43). We used a heat gun and broad scraper to remove most of the old paint on the large, flat surfaces. We scraped off loose, flaky paint before heat stripping (paint flakes can be ignited by a heat gun). Always use extra care near the edges of the woodwork to prevent damage to the wood and adjoining walls.

3 Chemically strip the intricate areas. Because a heat gun can scorch more delicate surfaces, we brushed a heavy layer of semi-paste chemical stripper onto the woodwork contours and edges. TIP: If your chemical stripper is not clinging well to vertical surfaces, try mixing some cornstarch into the stripper to thicken it.

4 Remove the stripper sludge. We used a specialty scraper (page 29) to scrape the contours in the door header and other trim areas. After removing most of the paint from these areas, we applied a thin layer of stripper to all the woodwork, then scrubbed with an abrasive pad to remove the remaining finish materials.

(continued next page)

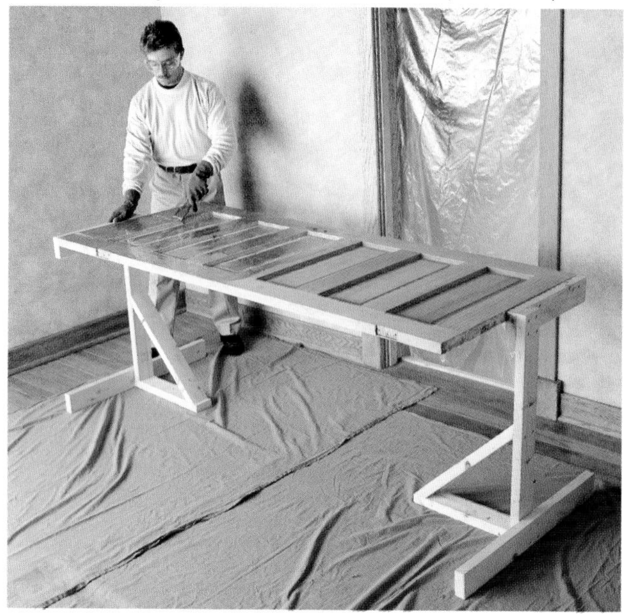

5 Strip the door. We removed all the door hardware, then stripped off the old finish using the same sequence of techniques we used for the woodwork: heat stripping, then chemical stripping and scraping. Because our refinishing plan included several doors, we built special door standards that allowed us to flip the door and work on the opposite side while one side dried. If you are only refinishing one or two doors, a pair of sturdy sawhorses is all you really need.

6 Clean the woodwork and door. We scrubbed all the wood surfaces with an abrasive pad dipped in mineral spirits. This removed the wax residue left by the chemical stripper, as well as a few traces of the old varnish.

7 Prepare for the finish (pages 52 to 57). We used stainable wood putty to fill the holes and gouges in the door and the woodwork. Then, after sanding, we tinted the putty with stain so it matched the color of the surrounding wood.

8 Sand the woodwork and door. We used a hand-sander with 150-grit sandpaper to even out the wood surfaces, then finish-sanded with 220-grit sandpaper, using a variety of grips and sanding blocks (page 29) to prepare the surface.

9 Color the wood (pages 58 to 63). It was not easy to find a combination of stain colors that gave us uniform results on the different wood types. But after some experimentation on pieces of scrap wood (and a little blending of stain colors), we settled on a light oak stain for the fir door, which absorbs stain more deeply than the woodwork. For the oak woodwork, we used the same oak stain, but mixed in a little walnut to darken the color.

10 Apply a topcoat (pages 70 to 73). We used tung oil because it is so easy to apply to details and is a very effective product for vertical surfaces. Three coats of tung oil gave us a hard, durable finish that was not overly glossy.

11 Make the finishing touches. After chemically stripping and cleaning the hardware (pages 80 to 82), we drilled new pilot holes, then reattached the hardware. We mounted the hinges on the door jamb, then hung the door, starting with the top hinge pin. Finally, we remounted all the switchplates and receptacle plates.

Case Studies

Wood Floor

Wood type: Red oak

Old finish: Medium oak stain with varnish and floor wax

Challenge: Completely remove worn, uneven finish

Solution: Sand down to bare wood with a drum sander and edger

Refinishing wood floors is one of the most popular do-it-yourself projects today, and for good reason. Few projects offer such a dramatic reward for a relatively small investment of time and money. The many scratches and the uneven wear on the floor shown here left us no option but to resurface. Many floors, however, do not need sanding. Sometimes stripping the old topcoat and applying a fresh finish is all it takes, so we included a chemical stripping variation (page 121).

Case Study: Wood Floor

1 Prepare the floor and room. We countersunk a few nails and screws so they were about ¼" below the floor surface, then we removed some staples so they would not tear our sandpaper. We also masked off doorways and ductwork to keep the sand and dust in our work area. Finally, we vacuumed the floor to remove dust.

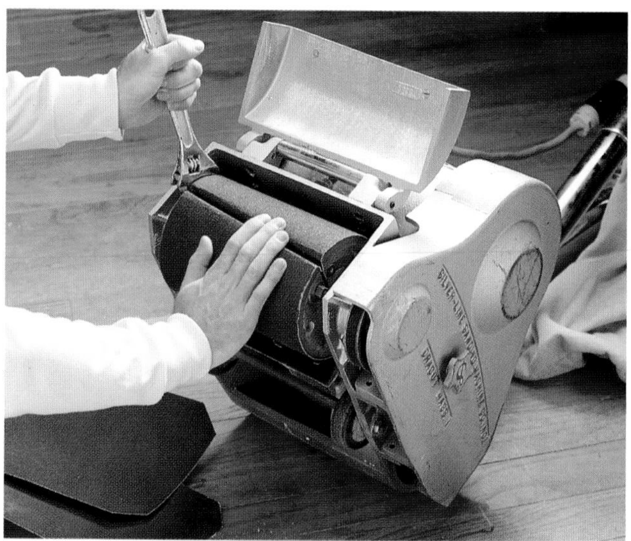

2 Prepare the equipment. We rented a drum sander and installed 80-grit sandpaper. (Make sure you get the rental store attendant to show you how to use the machines and replace sanding belts.) Because we had never used this sander, we tested it out on a sheet of plywood until we were comfortable using the machine.

3 Start sanding the floor. We positioned our drum sander in the center of the room, about 6" out from the wall. With the sanding drum in raised position, we turned on the machine and began moving it forward, lowering the drum as the sander moved. We sanded a straight path, following the direction of the floorboards and keeping the machine moving constantly.

4 Complete the first pass. We sanded to within about 1 ft. of the end wall in our first sanding pass, raising the drum as we neared the corner. NOTE: If the sandpaper clogs quickly or leaves quite a bit of finish intact, switch to a coarser grit—but as a general rule, use the finest grit that is effective for the job.

5 Make a second sanding pass. We repositioned the sander at our starting point so the next path overlapped the first by one-half its width. We sanded a second pass using the same method. Replacing the sandpaper as needed, we sanded overlapping paths all the way to the other side wall, then turned around and sanded the other half of the room.

6 Switch to finer sandpaper. After sanding with 80-grit paper, we switched to 120-grit for the second sanding stage. NOTE: Most of the old finish should be gone, as in the photo above, before you switch sandpaper grits. We made additional passes with 150-grit and 180-grit sandpaper.

(continued next page)

7 Sand the borders. We rented an edger to sand off the finish from the border areas of the floor. TIP: When you turn on the edger, make sure the sandpaper is not resting on the floor, and maintain light, even pressure on the machine as you work. Use the same sequence of sandpaper grits you used with the drum sander.

8 Scrape or sand the hard-to-reach areas. We used a sharp scraper to resurface our floor in awkward areas that could not be reached with a power sander. We used a finishing sander with 180-grit paper to feather out any remaining uneven areas and sanding ridges.

9 Apply a topcoat (pages 70 to 79). We used water-based polyurethane on our floor because its short drying time means less time for dust to settle into the finish. To apply the topcoat, we used a painting pad with a pole extension. Three thin coats gave us a durable finish. We buffed the dried finish with a fine abrasive pad to smooth out the surface.

Floor Variation: Chemically Strip a Wood Floor

1 Apply chemical stripper (pages 42 to 43). We were careful not to apply stripper over more floor area than we could scrape in 30 minutes (the active working time of the stripper we used). A 2 ft.-wide, 6 ft.-long area is a good working size.

2 Scrape off the stripper and old finish. We used a nylon stripper knife to remove the sludge, making sure to scrape in the same direction as the grain in the floorboards. Old newspaper was handy for depositing the sludge. We repeated steps 1 and 2 for the rest of the floor.

3 Scrub the floor. A medium abrasive pad dipped in mineral spirits removed residue left by the stripper, as well as the dissolved topcoat finish.

4 Clean out gaps between floorboards. Whenever you chemically strip a floor, the gaps and joints in the floor fill up with stripper and old finish. Left in the gaps, these chemicals can destroy your new topcoat. We simply scraped the old sludge out of the gaps with a palette knife.

5 Sand out stains. Even if there are several stains or discolored areas in your floorboards, you can avoid resurfacing the entire floor by carefully sanding out the problem areas, then feathering the edges of the sanded area. Bleach and oxalic acid are effective on some stains (pages 54 to 55).

6 Touch up with stain. The trick to this step is matching the old stain color. We found a medium oak stain that was almost identical to the original, and we used it to color a few bare-wood areas. After the stain dried, we applied three coats of water-based polyurethane (see step 9, page opposite).

Rub out white water spots with fine pumice powder and mineral spirits. First, clean the discolored area with a cloth dipped in mineral spirits. Next, sprinkle fine pumice powder onto the water spots. Dip a felt pad or soft cloth in mineral spirits as a lubricant, then buff the pumice powder until the water spots are gone. Recoat waxed surfaces with paste wax.

Maintenance & Quick Fixes

Refinishing furniture, a floor, or woodwork is a major investment of time and money. Protect your investment with a regular wood maintenance program, and avoid refinishing again by mastering a few quick fixes for minor finish problems. A basic wood maintenance program includes regular cleaning and dusting, and applying fresh paste wax or lemon oil. Repair scratches, scuffs, dents, and other minor surface flaws as they occur.

Everything You Need:

Tools: paint brushes, touch-up markers, putty knives, craft knife, candle, iron.

Materials: solvents, stain, topcoat materials, lemon oil, sandpaper, abrasive pads, fine pumice powder, shellac resin sticks, staining cloths, wood glue.

Wood Maintenance & Repair Kits

Packaged refinishing kits, sold at most building centers and paint stores, promise to refurbish a finish with no messy stripping. These products are sometimes successful on thicker topcoats with minor problems, but test them before using them on your fine furniture. Most kits contain a solvent for dissolving finishes, a topcoat product, and abrasive pads.

A wood maintenance kit should include basic tools, like paint brushes and putty knives, as well as any specialty tools that are useful for your furniture. Keep your tools together in a tool box, along with chemical solvents and samples of the stains and topcoats you have used on your wood.

Tips for Making Quick Fixes

Reattach splinters. Scrape any debris from the splintered area, then coat both surfaces with wood glue. Press the splinter back into place and secure with masking tape until the glue dries.

Resecure loose veneer. Cover the loosened veneer with a damp cloth, then press with a household iron set to a low temperature. Keep the iron moving and do not iron for more than a few seconds. Wait for the veneer glue to liquefy, then remove the iron and cloth. Before the glue rehardens, roll with a seam roller (page 29). Set a heavy book on the repair as it cools. If ineffective, reglue the veneer (pages 50 to 51).

How to Clean Finished Surfaces

1 Rub mineral spirits onto the wood surfaces to remove grime and wax buildup. Wipe off the mineral spirits and any dissolved wax with a fine abrasive pad. Repeat until all the wax is gone.

2 Apply a new coat of paste wax (pages 78 to 79). When the wax becomes filmy, buff with a clean, lint-free cloth. Apply another coat of paste wax after 24 hours. Renew the paste-wax topcoat at least once a year.

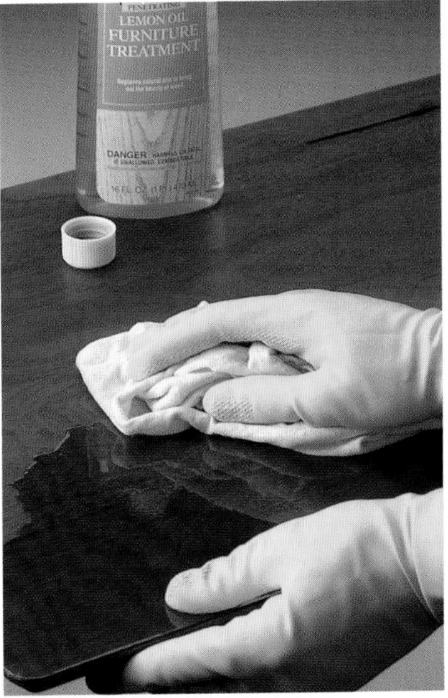

Option: Freshen dull or dry oil finishes using lemon oil. As an oil finish ages, essential oils are lost from the wood due to evaporation, wear, and cleaning. A coat of lemon oil restores these oils.

How to Blend Out Minor Finish Problems

Blend out minor finish problems in pure varnish (no synthetic additives), lacquer, or shellac finishes (pages 22 to 23) with a mixture of solvent and fresh topcoat material. First, clean dirt and wax from the problem area, then dissolve the finish using the right solvent mixture for each topcoat: **for pure varnish finishes (left)** mix one part clear tung oil to two parts mineral spirits; **for lacquer finishes (center)** use a 100% solution of lacquer thinner to liquefy the old lacquer; **for shellac finishes (right)** mix one part shellac to four parts denatured alcohol. Once the solvent mixture has liquefied the finish, gently brush or wipe the finish problem until it is smooth and evenly blended with the rest of the topcoat. For best results, apply a coat or two of paste wax over the entire surface once the repaired topcoat is dry. NOTE: Polymerized topcoats, like polyurethane, cannot be dissolved and repaired with this technique.

How to Repair Scuffs & Shallow Scratches

1 Wash the scratched or scuffed area thoroughly with a clean cloth and mineral spirits. Check to see if the damage has penetrated to the color layer, exposing bare wood.

OPTION: If the color layer has been damaged, use matching wood stain or a touch-up marker to color the exposed wood. If using stain, make sure the stain is compatible with the original finish (page 59). Allow the stain to dry.

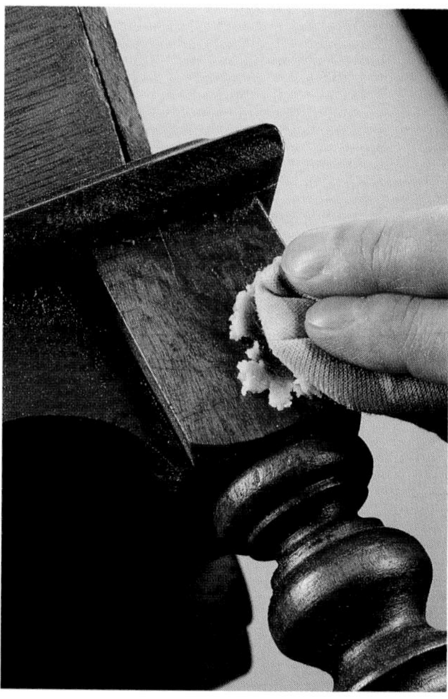

2 Lightly blend the area around the scratch with the solvent solution appropriate for the type of finish being repaired (see above). After the finish dries, apply paste wax over the entire surface (pages 78 to 79).

How to Repair Deep Scratches with a Shellac Resin Stick

1 Clean the area around the scratch with mineral spirits and a fine abrasive pad. Select a shellac resin stick that closely matches the finish color (if you cannot find an exact match, use a slightly lighter one).

2 Warm the tip of a putty knife over a candle flame. Use the hot knife to slice off a small piece of shellac resin from the stick. Let the resin melt on the knife blade.

3 Spread the molten resin on the damaged area, working it into the scratch with the putty knife. Let the resin harden, then reheat the knife and scrape off excess resin by pulling the flat edge of the warm knife across the resin mound until it is level with the wood surface.

4 Lightly sand the repaired area with 600-grit wet/dry sandpaper until the resin is level with the surface of the finish. Extend dark grain lines through the resin patch using a touch-up marker, then use a fine abrasive pad to apply paste wax to the repair. Buff with a clean cloth when dry.

Index

A

Accessories,
- *see:* Hardware & accessories

Alligatored finish, 19, 22-23
Aluminum oxide sandpaper, 53
Antiques,
- determining age, 17
- evaluating for refinishing, 17, 19, 104
- mantel clock case study, 104-105
- radio console case study, 110-111

B

Basswood, 26
Belt sander, 28
- loop sander, 28, 39
- to remove commercial finish, 38
- to resurface flat surface, 19, 102
- using, 39, 108

Birch, 26
Bird's-eye maple, 27
Bleaching wood to remove stains, 55, 121
Broken parts of furniture, repairing, 46-49
Brushes,
- cleaning, 33
- for chemical strippers, 43
- storing, 32-33
- types, 29

Burn marks,
- evaluating, 19
- repairing, 54

C

Cabinets,
- frame-and-panel cabinet case study, 100-101
- kitchen cabinet case study, 92-93
- music cabinet case study, 108-109
- sewing machine cabinet case study, 90-91

Cedar, 27
Cedar chest case study, 102-103
Chair, repairing, 94
Chemical stripping, 12, 36, 98, 101, 108, 113-115, 121
- heat sanding prior to, 40
- mixing with cornstarch for vertical surfaces, 115
- safety precautions, 23, 30-33
- sanding and scraping prior to, 38
- technique, 43
- to test old finishes, 23
- types of chemical strippers, 42
- wood floors, 20

Cherry, 27
Chest of drawers case study, 96-97
Cleaning finished surfaces, 123
Cleanup, 30-33
- vegetable oil to clean hands, 33

Clock, antique mantel, case study, 104-105
Color wash, 68-69
Coloring wood, 13, 24, 58-69
- *see also:* Painting, Staining

Commercial finishes,
- evaluating, 23
- removing, 38

Commercial stripping, 21
- preparing for, 37

Contours, stripping, 42-43, 88, 101, 115
Cracks,
- evaluating, 19
- repairing, 48, 103, 109

Crazed finish, 22-23
Crevices, sanding, 39, 88

D

Danish oil,
- *see:* Penetrating oil

Decorative painting, 68-69, 103
Denatured alcohol,
- to remove shellac, 42
- to test old finishes, 23
- use after chemical stripping, 42

Dents,
- evaluating, 19
- repairing, 13, 52, 54

Desk case study, 98-99
Detailed areas, stripping, 88, 101
Dining chair case study, 94-95
Disposal of refinishing materials, 30-33
Door & woodwork case study, 114-117
Double-hung window case study, 112-113
Drawer case study, 96-97
Drum sander, 118
Dry wood, refreshing, 109

E

Environmental concerns,
- and chemical strippers, 42
- and wood stains, 59
- disposal of refinishing supplies, 30, 32-33
- recycling old furniture, 6

Epoxy glue, 45
- making epoxy nails, 46, 94

Epoxy paint, removing, 38
Evaluating project, 12, 16-23
- furniture, 17-19
- wood floors, 20
- woodwork, 21

F

Farmhouse finish, 68
Finish,
- clear finishes, 27
- dark finishes, 26
- evaluating original, 16-17, 19, 22-23
- light finishes, 26
- painted finishes, 27
- removing old, 12, 36-43
- selecting new, 24-27

Finishing sander, 28, 93, 97, 102, 108
Finish sanding, 13, 38, 52, 56-57
- technique, 57

Fire extinguisher types, 31
Flat surface,
- repairing, 48, 99, 103
- resurfacing, 19, 102

Floors,
- *see:* Wood floors

Floor sander, 38, 118
Frame-and-panel cabinet case study, 100-101
Furniture,
- applying polyurethane, 76
- disassembling, 37
- evaluating refinishing project, 17-19
- repairing, 44-51

G

Garnet sandpaper, 53
Gel wood stains, 58-59, 107
- how to apply, 63

Glass, removing and reinstalling, 83, 105
Glue for wood repair, 45
Gluelines, repairing, 109
Gluing,
- flat surfaces, 48
- removing old glue, 45, 47
- spindles, legs or rungs, 49
- tools, 45
- veneer, 51

Gouges, repairing, 13, 52, 54-55, 102, 116
Grain, enhancing, 25-26
Grain filler, 24-25, 57, 106
- how to apply, 57

H
Hardware & accessories, 37
cleaning, 81, 91, 105, 109, 117
refurbishing, 13, 37, 81, 103
removing and reattaching, 82, 115, 117
replacing, 13, 80, 93, 97, 103
Hardwoods,
open-grained, 24, 52
sealing before final finishing, 52
Heat gun, 28, 90, 113, 115
how to use, 41
Heat stripping, 12, 36, 40-41, 113-115
sanding and scraping prior to, 38, 40-41
technique, 41
Holes, repairing, 27, 116

J
Joints,
disassembling, 47, 96
repairing, 46, 96

K
Kitchen cabinets case study, 92-93
Knot, repairing, 27
Knotty pine, 27

L
Lacquer,
identifying old lacquer, 23
removing, 40
repairing options, 23, 124
Lacquer thinner,
to remove old lacquer, 42
to repair finish, 23, 124
to test old finishes, 23
Lead-based finish,
disposal of residue, 32
identifying, 22
Leg, repairing, 49
Liquid wood stains, 58-59
how to apply, 62
Loop sander, 28, 39

M
Mahogany, 26
grain filler for, 24
sealing before final finishing, 52
Maple, 26
absorption of stain, 25
Masking, 105
hardware, 82
prior to coloring, 60, 67, 99, 103, 111
prior to removing finish, 37, 110, 112
work area, 115, 118
Mending plate, 46, 48
Mineral spirits,
reusing, 33
to remove wax buildup, 20, 22-23, 42, 123
to test old finishes, 23
Music cabinet case study, 108-109

N
Nicks, repairing, 54-55, 103

O
Oil-based paint, 65
see also: Painting
Oil finish,
identifying old finish, 23
freshening with lemon oil, 123
repairing options, 23
Old finish,
see: Finish
Orange cast on old finish, 23

P
Paint, removing, 38, 40, 42, 88, 90, 113-115
see also: Sanding, Scraping, Stripping
Painting, 13, 24, 64-69, 113
applying paint, 66-67
brushes for, 65
decorative painting, 68-69
identifying lead-based paint, 22
preparing wood for, 66
types of paint, 64-65
when to paint rather than strip, 18, 21, 27, 64
Parquet floors, 20
Paste wax, 24, 70-71, 103, 107, 109, 123
how to apply, 78-79
Penetrating oil, 24, 58-60, 111
how to use, 61
Pine, 26-27
absorption of stain, 25
sealing after finish sanding, 52
Plywood, 27
Polishing bonnet for power drill, 28, 78, 107
Polyurethane, 24, 70-71, 97, 111, 120-121
applying, 67, 74-77
identifying old finish, 23
removing, 36, 42, 98
repairing options, 23
storing, 72
types, 71
Poplar, 26
Primer, 66-67, 93, 99
Putty,
see: Wood putty

R
Radio console, antique, case study, 110-111
Random-orbit sander, 28, 52
Red oak, 26
absorption of stain, 25
grain filler for, 24
Refinishing process overview, 12-13
Repairing project, 12, 44-51
Reupholstering, 83, 95
Rocking chair case study, 88-89
Rubbing oil,
see: Penetrating oil
Rung, repairing, 49

S
Safety, 30-33
equipment, 31
Sanding, 12, 36, 38-39
finish sanding, 13, 38, 52, 56-57
tools, 28-29, 38-39
wood floors, 20, 118-120
Sanding block, 29, 39
Sanding cord, 39, 89
Sanding grip, 29, 39
Sanding sealer, 24-25, 52, 56-57, 97
making, 53
when to apply, 57, 60, 103, 113
Sandpaper types, 53
School desk case study, 98-99
Scraping, 36, 38-39, 115
tools, 28-29, 39, 91
Scratches, repairing, 44, 52, 54-55, 102-103, 124-125
Scuffs, repairing, 124
Seal coat, 24
Seat of chair, repairing, 46, 48
Sewing machine cabinet case study, 90-91
Shellac,
alligatored, 19, 23
identifying old shellac, 22-23
removing, 96, 100, 102, 104, 108, 111
repairing options, 22-23, 124
Shellac crayon, 125
Softwoods, 24
sealing after finish sanding, 52
selecting finish, 26-27
Spindle, repairing, 49
Splinter, reattaching, 44, 123
Staining, 13, 58-63
applying gel stain, 63
applying liquid stain, 62
preparing surface, 13, 60, 62
see also: Wood stain
Stains, removing, 52, 54-55, 121
Stenciling, 68-69, 99
Stripping,
when to paint rather than strip, 18, 21, 27, 64
see also: Chemical stripping, Commercial stripping, Heat stripping
Structural soundness, evaluating, 18

T
Table, tip-top, case study, 106-107
Tip-top table case study, 106-107
Tools for refinishing, 28-29

Topcoating, 13, 24, 70-79
applying, 70, 72, 74-79
evaluating original, 22-23, 36
preparing surface for, 13
types, 71
Tung oil, 24, 61, 70-71, 91, 105, 109, 117
applying, 73
storing, 72

V
Varnish, 107
identifying old finish, 23
removing, 40, 42, 88, 92, 94, 114-115
repairing options, 23, 124
Veneer, 90, 100
evaluating, 19, 50
ironing, 50, 123
repainting veneered piece, 18
repairing, 37, 44, 50-51, 101, 104, 123
veneered flooring, 20
Ventilation in work area, 30

W
Walnut, 27
grain pattern, 25
Water-based paint, 65
see also: Painting
Water stains,
evaluating, 19
removing, 122
Wax,
see: Paste wax
Wax buildup, removing, 20, 22-23, 42, 123
White oak, 26
Window, double-hung, case study, 112-113
disassembling, 112
Wood floors,
applying polyurethane, 77, 120
case study, 118-121
evaluating refinishing project, 20
removing wax buildup, 20, 22
repairing, 44
sanding, 38, 118-120
Wood grain filler, 52-53
Wood hardener, 21
Wood putty, 19, 27, 53, 89, 93, 95, 97, 99, 103, 109, 116
to replace missing veneer, 104
using, 54-55
Wood splinter, reattaching, 44
Wood stain, 24, 58-63
gel type, 58-59, 63, 107
oil-based liquid, 58-59, 62
selecting, 58-59
using, 60-63
water-based liquid, 58-59, 62
Wood sweller, 46, 89
Wood type and condition,
evaluating, 16-21, 24
Woodwork,
evaluating refinishing project, 21
repairing, 44-51
woodwork & door case study, 114-117

Y
Yellow cast on old finish, 23

Z
Zebrawood, 27

Product Information:

If you have difficulty finding any of the following materials featured in this book, call the manufacturers and ask for the name of the nearest sales representatives. The representatives can direct you to local retailers that stock these useful products.

Finish-removal products
Klean-Strip, a division of WM Barr
telephone: 1-800-235-3546

3M
telephone: 1-800-364-3577

Finishing products
The Bartley Collection Ltd.
telephone: 1-800-787-2800

Hardware Catalogue Companies
The Garret-Wade Tool Catalog
telephone: 1-800-221-2942

The Renovator's Supply
telephone: 1-800-659-0203

The Woodworker's Store
telephone: 1-800-279-4441